Grammar and Punctuation

Grammar 4 Teacher's Guide

Carol Matchett

Schofield&Sims

Free downloads available from the Schofield & Sims website

A selection of free downloads is available from the Schofield & Sims website (www.schofieldandsims.co.uk/free-downloads). These may be used to further enhance the effectiveness of the programme. The downloads add to the range of print materials supplied in the teacher's guides. They include the following items:

- a **Curriculum coverage chart**
- an enlarged **Focus text** for each lesson
- a **Dictation assessment sheet**
- a **Pupil target reminder**
- a **Learning pathways class chart** for each year group
- a **Final test analysis class chart** for each year group.

Published by **Schofield & Sims Ltd**, 7 Mariner Court, Wakefield, West Yorkshire WF4 3FL, UK
Telephone 01484 607080
www.schofieldandsims.co.uk

This edition copyright © Schofield & Sims Ltd, 2017
First published in 2017
Second impression 2018

Author: **Carol Matchett**
Carol Matchett has asserted her moral rights under the Copyright, Designs and Patents Act, 1988, to be identified as the author of this work.

British Library Cataloguing in Publication Data
A catalogue record for this book is available from the British Library.

Design by **Oxford Designers & Illustrators Ltd**

Printed in the UK by **Page Bros (Norwich) Ltd**

ISBN 978 07217 1397 7

Contents

INTRODUCTION   4

TEACHING NOTES AND ANSWERS

Section 1   Lesson 1   Extending sentences   10
                   Lesson 2   Subordinate clauses   12
                   Lesson 3   Word classes   14
                   Lesson 4   Determiners   16
                   Lesson 5   Noun phrases 1   18
                   Lesson 6   Noun phrases 2   20
                   Lesson 7   Punctuating direct speech 1   22
                   Lesson 8   Punctuating direct speech 2   24
                   Lesson 9   Pronouns within sentences   26
                   Lesson 10   Pronouns across sentences   28
                   Revision 1   30
                   Writing task 1   Analysis sheet   32
                                     Pupil checklist   33

Section 2   Lesson 11   Adverbials   34
                   Lesson 12   Fronted adverbials   36
                   Lesson 13   Commas after fronted adverbials   38
                   Lesson 14   Fronting subordinate clauses   40
                   Lesson 15   Singular and plural nouns   42
                   Lesson 16   Plural –s or possessive –'s?   44
                   Lesson 17   Apostrophes for plural possession 1   46
                   Lesson 18   Apostrophes for plural possession 2   48
                   Lesson 19   Standard English   50
                   Lesson 20   Verbs: perfect form   52
                   Revision 2   54
                   Writing task 2   Analysis sheet   56
                                     Pupil checklist   57

Section 3   Lesson 21   Possessive pronouns   58
                   Lesson 22   Making pronouns clear   60
                   Lesson 23   Co-ordinating and subordinating conjunctions   62
                   Lesson 24   Giving reasons: cause and effect   64
                   Lesson 25   Paragraphs: non-fiction   66
                   Lesson 26   Paragraphs: stories   68
                   Lesson 27   Negative sentences   70
                   Lesson 28   Questions and question tags   72
                   Lesson 29   Adjectives with prefixes and suffixes   74
                   Lesson 30   Word families   76
                   Revision 3   78
                   Writing task 3   Analysis sheet   80
                                     Pupil checklist   81

FINAL TEST   Final test   82
                   Mark scheme   86
                   Analysis sheet   88

TRACKING PROGRESS Target tracking sheet   89
                   Learning pathways sheet   90

GLOSSARY   91

Introduction

Schofield & Sims Grammar and Punctuation is a structured whole-school scheme for teaching grammar and punctuation while also building on vocabulary, reading and writing skills. It can be used alongside the **Schofield & Sims Spelling** series for complete Spelling, Punctuation and Grammar [SPaG] coverage.

Grammar and Punctuation is designed to progressively develop knowledge and understanding of grammatical concepts through six teacher's guides and six pupil books containing a carefully structured sequence of lessons. The teacher's guides provide you, the teacher or adult helper, with notes and activities to support the teaching of these lessons, annotated answers to the pupil book questions, and a variety of assessment resources for tracking progress.

Supporting a mastery approach, the focus of this programme is on rich practice, deep and secure understanding and fluency in application. Pupils not only learn the terminology and correct usage of grammar and punctuation, but they also build up the skills, knowledge and confidence to apply them in their own independent writing. All pupils are encouraged to move at the same pace through the lessons and are given the same opportunity to fully understand the concept being taught. A wealth of practice questions, writing tasks, activity ideas and resources are provided to support the wider application of the grammar and punctuation that has been learnt in each lesson and to help pupils to truly master the art of writing.

The programme is designed primarily for pupils in Years 1 to 6, and the concepts and terminology that are introduced are in line with the National Curriculum for English. However, understanding of grammar and punctuation is cumulative, so grammatical terms and concepts introduced in one book are revisited and developed further in subsequent books to reinforce the pupils' understanding. In particular, concepts and areas of learning introduced towards the end of one book are revisited and embedded in the next book to further ensure consolidation and continuity.

There are 30 corresponding lessons in **Grammar 4** and its related **Teacher's Guide**, ten for each term. These lessons follow the statutory requirements for Year 4 'Vocabulary, grammar and punctuation' in the National Curriculum for English, including Appendix 2, while also promoting and supporting other aspects of the English curriculum. A curriculum coverage chart is available to download from the Schofield & Sims website. An extended glossary can also be found at the back of this teacher's guide [pages 91–96], with a full list of all the terminology relevant to the Year 4 curriculum, along with clear explanations, examples and lesson references.

IMPLEMENTING THE TEACHING MODEL

The **Grammar 4 Teacher's Guide** supports explicit teaching of grammar and punctuation within the wider teaching of reading, writing and speaking. It is based around focused teaching sessions, using the following pedagogical model:

Teach   Practise   Apply   Assess

USING THE TEACHING NOTES

This teacher's guide supports an approach to teaching grammar and punctuation that is systematic, thorough and direct. It provides you with detailed **Teaching notes** for each lesson. A sample page is included below to show the structure of a typical lesson.

Lesson 1 Extending sentences

Focus using prepositions and adverbs to add detail [where, when, how] to a main clause

Key terms adverb, preposition, main clause, sentence, noun, noun phrase, verb

Focus text The knight approached the cave with a heavy heart. He sighed anxiously. Then he paused for a moment at the entrance to the cave. Somewhere inside, shadows flickered in the gloom.

TEACH

Show the focus text and read it aloud. Discuss ideas about the character, setting and actions [e.g. Ask: What do you think the knight is doing? Why? How is he feeling? What might be in the cave?].

Read aloud the underlined parts of the sentences. Ask the pupils what they notice [e.g. they are main clauses; they make sense even without the other words; they could be complete sentences].

Read aloud the full sentences. Discuss what the additional words and phrases tell us [e.g. *how* he approached the cave; *when* and *where* he paused; *where* the shadows flickered].

Use the focus text to reinforce terms relating to sentences. Explain that a sentence must have at least one main clause – a group of words that communicates a complete idea and makes sense on its own. It contains a verb and usually a subject [e.g. he paused]. A phrase is a group of words that go together but with no verb – it is not a complete sentence. Ask the pupils to identify phrases in the focus text [e.g. with a heavy heart; for a moment; in the gloom].

Explain that we add words and phrases to a main clause to give extra detail about an event. We can add adverbs to say where [somewhere inside], when [then], how [anxiously] or how often. We can use prepositional phrases in the same way, to show where [at the entrance], when [for a moment] or how [with a heavy heart]. Remind the pupils that a preposition is followed by a noun or noun phrase [e.g. in the gloom] to make a prepositional phrase. Work with the pupils to add words and phrases to another main clause [e.g. There was a sound.].

Explain that we can also add an adverb to another adverb or to a prepositional phrase. The first adverb modifies the second [e.g. somewhere inside].

EXTEND Discuss adding adverbs and prepositional phrases to the start of a sentence as well as the end.

PRACTISE

Pupil book page 4

APPLY

- When writing stories and accounts, encourage the pupils to use adverbs and prepositional phrases to add more detail about where, when and how events happen.
- Remind the pupils to orally rehearse sentences before writing, trying out words and phrases.
- The pupils use adverbs and prepositional phrases in instructions to give detail about where, when and how [e.g. Put the ingredients in a mixing bowl. Mix them together with a fork.].
- The pupils write descriptions of places, using adverbs and prepositions to create an atmosphere.

ASSESS

Dictation: He arrived by train around midnight. He left the station straightaway. He walked home with tired footsteps.
Say: Underline the main clause in each sentence. What has been added to each main clause?
Answer: Phrases [e.g. by train] and adverbs [e.g. straightaway].

10

The learning objective of the lesson.

Terminology that the pupils will encounter in the lesson.

A short focus text for use at the start of the lesson.

Detailed lesson notes offering guidance on how to teach a specific grammatical feature or concept.

Extension of the lesson focus for pupils who want to explore further.

Reference to the relevant pupil book page, which contains practice activities to develop understanding.

A dictation activity to assess learning.

Ideas and activities for applying the concepts in speech and independent writing.

TEACH

Each lesson begins with an introductory panel featuring the following information:

- **Focus** – The focus of the lesson is clearly stated.
- **Key terms** – The key terminology to be used in the teaching session is listed. Any new terminology that the pupils will come across for the first time in that lesson is highlighted in bold.
- **Focus text** – A short focus text is provided that has been designed for use at the start of the lesson. It is intended that the focus text is written or projected on to a whiteboard to be shared with the pupils. The focus texts cover a range of genres of writing and help to provide a context for the learning that allows the pupils to appreciate the purpose or effect of the target grammar or punctuation feature. All the focus texts are available to download from the Schofield & Sims website.

Clear guidance is given on how to use the **Focus text** at the start of the lesson to 'focus in' on the particular grammar or punctuation feature that you are teaching. The **Teaching notes** suggest possible ways that you can explain, demonstrate and discuss the feature to develop understanding. Sessions often involve some oral composition or shared writing, with the pupils involved in suggesting ideas and correcting mistakes.

The main teaching session covers the objectives that are required for the pupils to work at the expected standard, but there is also a suggestion for how you can **Extend** the focus for pupils who have grasped the main concept and are ready to delve deeper. These suggestions often provide a bridge to later lessons in the programme.

PRACTISE

Following the teaching session, the pupils are ready to practise the grammar or punctuation feature that has been introduced, and clear page references are given for the corresponding lesson in the pupil book. This provides the pupils with rich practice activities to consolidate their learning. The pupils can work individually or in pairs. In paired work, discussion between partners can help to develop understanding, encourage thoughtful answers and promote oral rehearsal.

At the top of each pupil book page a **Remember** panel provides a child-friendly summary of a key learning point from the lesson, with examples that refer back to the **Focus text**. This acts as a reminder for the pupil and is also a useful reference for parents if sections of the pupil book are set as homework.

In **Grammar 4**, there are three pupil book activities for each lesson. The first **Try it** activity is designed to check that the pupils understand the key learning point; the second is designed to develop and use this understanding within sentences. You could do some of the activities orally, with the class or in groups, before the pupils write their answers. Each lesson then ends with a **Sentence practice** activity where the pupils compose their own sentence or sentences using the concept that has been taught in the lesson. If a pupil requires additional challenge, the **Sentence practice** could be extended by increasing the number of sentences required. A sample page from the pupil book is provided on page 7. It shows the structure of a typical page and some of the main features.

As the pupil book is completed, it will form an ongoing record of the pupil's progress. It will also be a useful reminder for the pupil when writing independently.

Answers to all the pupil book activities are provided in the teacher's guide. Alongside the answers you will also find detailed annotations offering guidance on what to look out for and how to tackle potential problems, as well as suggestions for discussing or comparing the pupils' answers.

There are **Revision** pages at the end of each section of the pupil book. In **Grammar 4**, these pages revise concepts introduced in earlier books as well as material from earlier sections of the current book, making sure that learning is not forgotten. The focus of each revision activity is given on the **Answers** pages in the teacher's guide to help you identify areas where the pupils might need further revision.

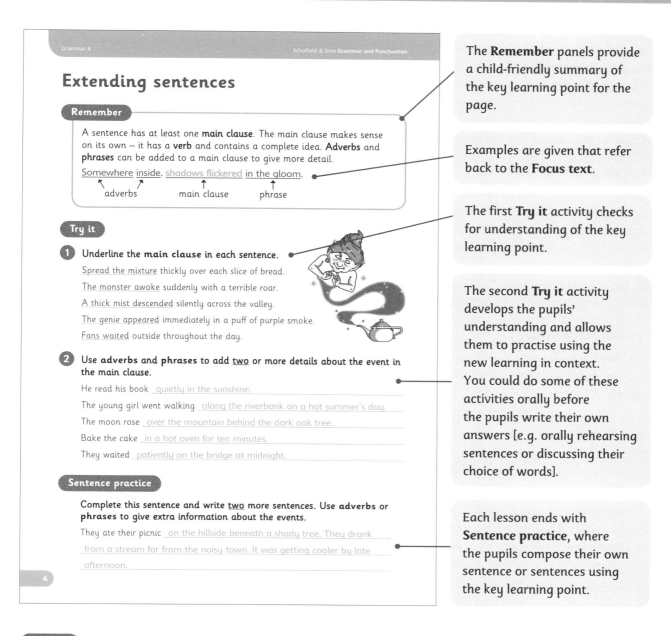

Grammar 4

Schofield & Sims **Grammar and Punctuation**

Extending sentences

Remember

A sentence has at least one **main clause**. The main clause makes sense on its own – it has a **verb** and contains a complete idea. **Adverbs** and **phrases** can be added to a main clause to give more detail.

Somewhere inside, shadows flickered in the gloom.

adverbs   main clause   phrase

Try it

1 Underline the **main clause** in each sentence.

Spread the mixture thickly over each slice of bread.

The monster awoke suddenly with a terrible roar.

A thick mist descended silently across the valley.

The genie appeared immediately in a puff of purple smoke.

Fans waited outside throughout the day.

2 Use **adverbs** and **phrases** to add **two** or more details about the event in the main clause.

He read his book _quietly in the sunshine._

The young girl went walking _along the riverbank on a hot summer's day._

The moon rose _over the mountain behind the dark oak tree._

Bake the cake _in a hot oven for ten minutes._

They waited _patiently on the bridge at midnight._

Sentence practice

Complete this sentence and write **two** more sentences. Use **adverbs** or **phrases** to give extra information about the events.

They ate their picnic _on the hillside beneath a shady tree. They drank_ _from a stream far from the noisy town. It was getting cooler by late_ _afternoon._

4

The **Remember** panels provide a child-friendly summary of the key learning point for the page.

Examples are given that refer back to the **Focus text**.

The first **Try it** activity checks for understanding of the key learning point.

The second **Try it** activity develops the pupils' understanding and allows them to practise using the new learning in context. You could do some of these activities orally before the pupils write their own answers [e.g. orally rehearsing sentences or discussing their choice of words].

Each lesson ends with **Sentence practice**, where the pupils compose their own sentence or sentences using the key learning point.

APPLY

A challenge when teaching grammar and punctuation is ensuring that pupils transfer learning from grammar lessons into their own writing. This is why the **Teaching notes** always provide a list of suggestions for activities where the pupils might apply their new learning in written, or sometimes oral, composition. These opportunities may be in English lessons or across the curriculum. You can use these suggestions as and when appropriate and you should also look for opportunities to embed learning in the writing activities you already have planned.

It is important to establish the expectation that what has been taught and practised in a grammar and punctuation lesson is applied when writing. This can be helped by setting targets for writing that relate to a specific grammar and punctuation concept that has been taught, and referring to these before, during and after writing, especially in marking and feedback. You will find further support for target-setting on page 9.

At the end of each section of the pupil book there is a short **Writing task**. This again helps to make explicit the link between the grammar and punctuation lessons and the pupils' own writing. The writing task provides an opportunity for the pupils to apply, or 'show off', what they have learnt about grammar and punctuation by using it in written composition. It can be used as a starting point for further creative writing or topic-based activities. There is more information about how to use and assess the **Writing task** on page 8.

ASSESS

Regular assessment is crucial to check understanding, reflect on learning and monitor progress. It is important that teachers know what the pupils have learnt, what they are finding difficult and what they need to know next. This helps inform teaching, planning and target-setting. **Grammar 4** and its related **Teacher's Guide** offer frequent opportunities and a range of resources for in-school assessment, which can be used flexibly in line with your own school's assessment policy.

Ongoing assessment

At the end of each page of the **Teaching notes** you will find a short assessment task based around a dictation exercise. This is designed to be used once pupils have completed the relevant lesson in the pupil book and begun to apply the new learning in their writing. The pupils are required to write and punctuate a dictated sentence or sentences. They are often then asked to change or annotate the sentences in some way, following verbal prompts. This dictation task is designed to show whether pupils have understood the terminology and the key learning objective of the lesson. Sometimes previous learning is also checked. A **Dictation assessment sheet** is available to download from the Schofield & Sims website.

Periodic assessment

The **Writing task** at the end of each section in the pupil book allows for a more formal assessment of how the pupils are applying their cumulative knowledge of sentence structure, grammar and punctuation in their own writing.

At Key Stage 2, the writing tasks require pupils to write for different purposes and in different forms. You can remind the pupils that you will be looking at their choices of vocabulary, grammar and punctuation but do not give any further help or examples of sentences, words or phrases that might affect the assessment. Allow the pupils a few minutes' planning time to note down their ideas before they begin writing.

Included in the teacher's guide is an **Analysis sheet** for each **Writing task** [pages 32, 56 and 80]. This lists relevant criteria relating to punctuation, and to grammar and sentence structure based on what has been taught to date. Look for each criterion in the pupil's completed **Writing task** and record whether there is no evidence, some evidence or clear evidence of the use of that feature in the piece of writing. Photocopies of these sheets can also be used to analyse other samples of writing to give a better picture of a pupil's abilities.

Also included is a **Pupil checklist** for each **Writing task** [pages 33, 57 and 81]. This is designed to encourage the pupils' self-assessment and also allows you to give targeted feedback. As the pupils complete the checklist you could ask them to annotate their writing to show where they have successfully used a particular grammar or punctuation feature [e.g. circling the conjunctions they have used].

Whether you choose to use the **Analysis sheet** or the **Pupil checklist**, both include a space for you to record a future target for the pupil. This is an important part of the writing assessments: identifying strengths and weaknesses and informing future teaching. Any problems or misunderstandings that are noted should be addressed and targets updated based on the evidence.

Summative assessment

There is a **Final test** provided as a photocopiable resource on pages 82–85 of this teacher's guide. This is designed to be used as an end-of-year assessment when all or most of the sections of the pupil book are complete. It is similar in style to the short answer test in the end of Key Stage 2 National Tests and it covers all the content introduced in the programme so far. You can use it to help check the pupils' learning and whether their progress is in line with expectations.

A **Mark scheme** for the **Final test** is provided on pages 86–87 and gives the answers and assessment focus of each question. The **Analysis sheet** for the **Final test** allows you to record the pupils' marks and will be helpful in identifying individual or class strengths and areas that might need to be revisited. This can be found on page 88 and a whole-class version is available to download from the Schofield & Sims website.

Tracking progress

A number of resources are provided at the back of the teacher's guide and as downloadable resources to further support assessment of learning, tracking progress and record-keeping.

Following a **Writing task**, if a group of pupils require further focused support on a particular writing target, the **Target tracking sheet** on page 89 can be used to note evidence of progress towards that target. You should look for evidence of progress in independent writing in English and in other subjects. Judgements should not be made solely on one piece of writing.

Pupil name	Evidence from independent writing	Progress in independent writing
Sarah Jacobs	Paragraph on 'My family'. Book review of 'The Nightingale'. Science report on 'Habitats'.	① ② ③

The target should be reviewed after a set period of time to see if it has been achieved. A new target might then be set, or further teaching and reinforcement opportunities planned as necessary. A **Pupil target reminder** is available to download from the Schofield & Sims website. This can be placed on a pupil's desk as a prompt to remind them of their current writing target.

The **Learning pathways sheet** on page 90 acts as an at-a-glance overview of where a pupil is in their learning. If completed at regular intervals [e.g. at the end of every term] it allows you to track the progress that has been made and to identify areas where further support might be needed. Alternatively, it can be completed just once at the end of the year to act as a useful summative record for the pupil's subsequent teacher. The chart shows criteria in line with the expected standards for Year 4. Circles are ticked to show the depth of a pupil's understanding. These judgements should be made using a variety of evidence, including a number of examples of independent writing. Learning is only definitely embedded when the concept is always or nearly always present, based on evidence from a range of writing tasks. A **Learning pathways class chart**, available to download from the Schofield & Sims website, allows you to keep a record of progress for the whole class in one spreadsheet.

The pupils should also be encouraged to reflect on their own learning at regular intervals, saying what they have learnt and how they have used it in their writing. There is a **Progress chart** at the back of the pupil book where the pupils can record their progress through the programme by ticking the circle when they feel they have achieved the content of the statement.

Lesson 1 Extending sentences

Focus using prepositions and adverbs to add detail [where, when, how] to a main clause

Key terms adverb, preposition, main clause, sentence, noun, noun phrase, verb

Focus text <u>The knight approached the cave</u> with a heavy heart. <u>He sighed</u> anxiously. Then <u>he paused</u> for a moment at the entrance to the cave. Somewhere inside, <u>shadows flickered</u> in the gloom.

TEACH

Show the focus text and read it aloud. Discuss ideas about the character, setting and actions [e.g. Ask: What do you think the knight is doing? Why? How is he feeling? What might be in the cave?].

Read aloud the underlined parts of the sentences. Ask the pupils what they notice [e.g. they are main clauses; they make sense even without the other words; they could be complete sentences].

Read aloud the full sentences. Discuss what the additional words and phrases tell us [e.g. *how* he approached the cave; *when* and *where* he paused; *where* the shadows flickered].

Use the focus text to reinforce terms relating to sentences. Explain that a sentence must have at least one main clause – a group of words that communicates a complete idea and makes sense on its own. It contains a verb and usually a subject [e.g. he paused]. A phrase is a group of words that go together but with no verb – it is not a complete sentence. Ask the pupils to identify phrases in the focus text [e.g. with a heavy heart; for a moment; in the gloom].

Explain that we add words and phrases to a main clause to give extra detail about an event. We can add adverbs to say where [somewhere inside], when [then], how [anxiously] or how often. We can use prepositional phrases in the same way, to show where [at the entrance], when [for a moment] or how [with a heavy heart]. Remind the pupils that a preposition is followed by a noun or noun phrase [e.g. <u>in</u> the gloom] to make a prepositional phrase. Work with the pupils to add words and phrases to another main clause [e.g. There was a sound.].

Explain that we can also add an adverb to another adverb or to a prepositional phrase. The first adverb modifies the second [e.g. somewhere inside].

EXTEND Discuss adding adverbs and prepositional phrases to the start of a sentence as well as the end.

PRACTISE

Pupil book page 4

APPLY

- When writing stories and accounts, encourage the pupils to use adverbs and prepositional phrases to add more detail about where, when and how events happen.
- Remind the pupils to orally rehearse sentences before writing, trying out words and phrases.
- The pupils use adverbs and prepositional phrases in instructions to give detail about where, when and how [e.g. Put the ingredients <u>in a mixing bowl</u>. Mix them together <u>with a fork</u>.].
- The pupils write descriptions of places, using adverbs and prepositions to create an atmosphere.

ASSESS

Dictation: <u>He arrived</u> by train around midnight. <u>He left the station</u> straightaway. <u>He walked</u> home with tired footsteps.
Say: Underline the main clause in each sentence. What has been added to each main clause?
Answer: Phrases [e.g. by train] and adverbs [e.g. straightaway].

Pupil book answers

Extending sentences

Remember

A sentence has at least one **main clause**. The main clause makes sense on its own – it has a **verb** and contains a complete idea. **Adverbs** and **phrases** can be added to a main clause to give more detail.

Somewhere inside, shadows flickered in the gloom.

adverbs   main clause   phrase

Try it

1 Underline the **main clause** in each sentence.

Spread the mixture thickly over each slice of bread.

The monster awoke suddenly with a terrible roar.

A thick mist descended silently across the valley.

The genie appeared immediately in a puff of purple smoke.

Fans waited outside throughout the day.

The pupils need to separate the main clause from any adverbs or prepositional phrases.

You could discuss what extra details the adverbs and prepositional phrases give [e.g. where, when and how].

These sentences provide useful models for completing the second activity.

2 Use **adverbs** and **phrases** to add two or more details about the event in the main clause.

He read his book quietly in the sunshine.

The young girl went walking along the riverbank on a hot summer's day.

The moon rose over the mountain behind the dark oak tree.

Bake the cake in a hot oven for ten minutes.

They waited patiently on the bridge at midnight.

These are just examples to show how adverbs and prepositional phrases might be used and combined. Look for extra detail about where, when or how, with sentences including, ideally, two added phrases or an adverb and a phrase. Use oral rehearsal to encourage careful choices. Compare the pupils' answers to discuss different effects.

Sentence practice

Complete this sentence and write two more sentences. Use **adverbs** or **phrases** to give extra information about the events.

They ate their picnic on the hillside beneath a shady tree. They drank from a stream far from the noisy town. It was getting cooler by late afternoon.

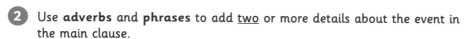

This is just an example. Look for the use of prepositional phrases and/ or adverbs to add extra detail about where, when or how, with sentences including, ideally, two added phrases or an adverb and a phrase. Compare the pupils' answers to discuss different ways sentences have been developed.

All sentences written by the pupils should now be correctly punctuated.

4

Lesson 2 Subordinate clauses

Focus adding subordinate clauses to main clauses; using a range of subordinating conjunctions

Key terms clause, main clause, subordinate clause, conjunction

Focus text <u>We have been trapped</u> since we were attacked. <u>I was not allowed to fight</u> as I am only nine years old. <u>We thought we were safe</u> after the battle ended. <u>We are alive</u> although the enemy is still out there. <u>We will starve</u> unless we get some supplies soon.

TEACH

Show the focus text and explain that the sentences are from a historical diary. Read it aloud. Discuss the events [e.g. What has happened? What is the situation now?].

Read aloud the underlined parts of the sentences. Ask the pupils what they notice [they are main clauses; they make sense without the rest of the sentence]. Discuss what the rest of the sentence adds [e.g. *when* they were trapped; *why* he was not allowed to fight; a contrast to them being alive]. Discuss how the extra information has been added [e.g. using a conjunction to add a subordinate clause].

Revise the term 'subordinate clause'. A subordinate clause is added to a main clause to give more detail about what the main clause tells us [e.g. when or why something happened]. It is subordinate because it is less important than the main clause. Explain that it does not make sense without the main clause but is still a clause, because it has a subject and a verb [e.g. since <u>we were attacked</u>].

Point out that subordinate clauses usually begin with a conjunction [e.g. since; as; after; although]. [Note: These conjunctions are called subordinating conjunctions. This term will be introduced in Lesson 23.] These can show time, cause [the reason why], or contrast. Some conjunctions such as 'since' and 'as' can be used to give information about either time *or* cause.

Invite the pupils to orally compose more sentences using a range of conjunctions [e.g. I was hiding while ...; We had plenty of food before ...; I am scared because ...; We tried to smile although ...].

EXTEND Discuss how words such as 'after' and 'since' can be prepositions or conjunctions depending on how they are used in a sentence [e.g. 'after the battle ended' – conjunction; 'after the battle' – preposition].

PRACTISE

Pupil book page 5

APPLY

- When reading with the pupils, look at the conjunctions used at the beginning of subordinate clauses in different types of text [e.g. in an argument compared to a diary or account].
- Display lists of conjunctions for the pupils to refer to when they are orally rephrasing sentences.
- When writing information texts, the pupils convert notes into complete sentences using conjunctions to link or expand on ideas. Encourage them to orally rehearse sentences before choosing the conjunctions.
- When writing stories, encourage the pupils to expand some sentences with subordinate clauses to give more detail about an event, but also to leave some short sentences for effect.

ASSESS

Dictation: I fetched the water <u>while Joseph gathered firewood</u>. We would need a fire <u>as it was getting dark</u>. I would feel safer <u>if there was a fire</u>.
Say: Underline the subordinate clause in each sentence.

Pupil book answers

Subordinate clauses

Remember

A **subordinate clause** can be added to a **main clause** to give more detail about an event. The subordinate clause has a **verb** but does not make sense without the main clause. A subordinate clause usually begins with a **conjunction** such as 'after', 'although' or 'as'.

We thought we were safe after the battle ended.

main clause   conjunction   subordinate clause

Remind the pupils that a subordinate clause starts with a conjunction and does not make sense by itself. You could discuss what the subordinate clause adds [e.g. detail about when, why or a contrast].

These are just examples. Discuss what extra information has been added to the main clause [e.g. 'as' can give detail about both time and cause].

Check that 'before' and 'until' have been used as conjunctions rather than prepositions [e.g. 'until morning' is a prepositional phrase, while 'until it was morning' is a subordinate clause].

Try it

1   Underline the **subordinate clause** in each sentence.

Kyle went into the house while Ashley waited outside.

We will plant the crops after the frost has gone.

We had to stop gardening as it was getting dark.

Ned nibbled at a biscuit although he wasn't really hungry.

Joe has been miserable since his friend went away.

2   Complete the **subordinate clause** in each sentence.

Yasmin licked her lips as she sat down at the table.

We cannot open the door unless we find the key.

Take the washing down before it starts to rain.

The mouse did not run away although she was scared of the cat.

The shop was nearly empty because it was almost five o'clock.

The little man stamped his foot until he made a hole in the floor.

Sentence practice

Write three sentences about arriving at a campsite, using **subordinate clauses** to give extra details.

It was beginning to rain when we arrived at the campsite. Mum said we

must pitch the tent as it was getting late. Dad made the frame while I

sorted out the canvas.

5

This is just an example of sentences on the given theme using subordinate clauses. Look for the use of different conjunctions to express time and cause.

Lesson 3 Word classes

Focus word classes; recognising words that function in different ways in different sentences

Key terms word classes, verb, noun, adjective, adverb, pronoun, preposition, conjunction

Focus text We wait for the start of the race.
Beth starts well and I race after her.
Beth is a fast runner. She always trains hard.
I will have to run fast to beat her. It will be a hard race.

TEACH

Show the first two sentences of the focus text and read them aloud. Discuss what the pupils notice about the highlighted words. Ask: What type of words are they? [the same words, 'start' and 'race', appear in both sentences but they are nouns in the first sentence and verbs in the second]

Show and read aloud the rest of the focus text. Discuss what the pupils notice about the highlighted words this time [the words 'hard' and 'fast' are used as adjectives to describe a noun – 'a fast runner', and as adverbs to describe a verb – 'run fast'].

Explain that we group words into different word classes. The pupils will be familiar with seven of the main word classes: verb, noun, adjective, adverb, pronoun, preposition, conjunction. [Note: The eighth word class, determiner, is introduced in the next lesson, Lesson 4.]. Remind them that these word classes describe how the words are used in sentences [e.g. nouns name things; adjectives describe nouns; pronouns stand in place of nouns]. Ask the pupils to identify words in the focus text that belong to some of these word classes [e.g. pronoun – 'we', 'I', 'her', 'she'; preposition – 'for', 'of', 'after'].

Some words can belong to more than one word class depending on how they are used in a sentence, as shown by the focus text. Explain that we must look at how and where a word is used in a sentence to know which word class it belongs to [e.g. 'hard' is an adjective if used with a noun; an adverb if used with a verb].

EXTEND Discuss words that can be both prepositions and conjunctions. A word is a preposition if followed by a noun or pronoun [e.g. I race after her.]; a conjunction if followed by a subordinate clause [e.g. I race after the others finish.].

PRACTISE

Pupil book page 6

APPLY

- The pupils use dictionaries to look at how an entry shows different word meanings and word classes.
- In other curriculum areas, encourage the pupils to look for words that can be used in different ways – for example, as verbs and nouns [e.g. to reserve/a nature reserve; to cycle/a cycle].
- The pupils use the names of word classes when noting ideas before writing [e.g. in descriptions – adverbs to describe movements, nouns to name parts or things seen].
- When reading with the pupils, look for words that can be used as adjectives *or* adverbs and discuss how they are used in that particular sentence.

ASSESS

Dictation: Katie went first. I knew she would be a hard act to follow.
Say: Is the word 'act' a noun or a verb? Is the word 'hard' an adjective or an adverb?
Answer: 'act' a noun; 'hard' an adjective

Pupil book answers

Word classes

Remember

Words can be grouped into different **word classes** such as **verbs**, **nouns**, **adjectives** and **adverbs**. Some words can belong to more than one word class, depending on how they are used in a sentence.

Beth is a fast runner. (adjective – describing a noun)

I will have to run fast to beat her. (adverb – describing a verb)

Try it

1   Read each sentence. Is the underlined word an **adjective** or an **adverb**?

It was a hard climb.   adjective

We all worked hard and did our best.   adverb

The number five bus arrived late today.   adverb

We had a late lunch today.   adjective

He had to cross a wide river.   adjective

Suddenly, the doors opened wide.   adverb

2   Write two sentences using the word 'play' first as a **verb** and then as a **noun**.

verb   I sometimes play snakes and ladders with my brother.

noun   We are putting on a play for our parents.

Now write two sentences using the word 'break' first as a **verb** and then as a **noun**.

verb   The plate will break if you drop it.

noun   I will take a break after I finish my homework.

Sentence practice

Write two sentences using the word 'early' first as an **adjective** and then as an **adverb**.

adjective   Ryan caught the early train.

adverb   He arrived home early.

6

If the pupils find this difficult, remind them to look at where and how the word is used in the sentence:

- Is it directly before a noun? Does it tell us about the noun? [e.g. a hard climb]. If yes, then it is an adjective.
- Is it after or close to a verb? Does it tell us more about the verb? [e.g. worked hard] If yes, then it is an adverb.

These are examples of sentences showing different functions of the words. Check that the first sentence uses the word as a verb and the second as a noun.

These are examples of sentences showing the word 'early' used as an adjective and an adverb.

Lesson 4 Determiners

Focus introducing the term 'determiner'; using determiners to specify nouns

Key terms **determiner**, noun, noun phrase

Focus text This cat sleeps in the sun. That cat sleeps in the dark.
Some cats sleep on a rug. Many cats sleep by a fire.
Your cat sleeps in her basket. Our cat sleeps on my lap.

TEACH

Show the focus text and read it aloud. Discuss the highlighted words at the start of each sentence and how they change the subject of the sentence. Ask the pupils if each sentence is about a specific cat [this cat, that cat, your cat, our cat] or about cats in general [some cats, many cats].

Explain that the highlighted words are called determiners. A determiner comes before a noun or at the start of a noun phrase. A noun phrase could just be a determiner and a noun [e.g. our cat]. If adjectives are added, the determiner still comes at the start of the noun phrase [e.g. our little cat]. There are some other determiners in the focus text that are not highlighted. Ask the pupils to identify them. Remind them to look for words before nouns [the sun/dark, a rug/fire, her basket, my lap].

Explain that the job of the determiner is to specify the noun [e.g. say which cat is being referred to]. It can point to a specific cat [e.g. this cat; that cat] or refer to cats generally [e.g. many cats].

The most common determiners are the words 'the', 'a' and 'an' [called articles] but, as the focus text shows, many other words also function as determiners. Words like 'some' and 'many' are quantifiers that define *how many*. Words like 'this' and 'that' point to a *specific cat* [or group of cats – 'these', 'those']. Some determiners are possessives defining *whose cat* [e.g. your cat; our cat]. These words are often thought of as pronouns but if they come before a noun they function as determiners.

Invite the pupils to orally compose some more sentences, using other determiners before the noun 'cat/s'. [e.g. All cats ...; Both cats ...; Few cats ...; Those cats ...; These cats ...; Their cat ...; His cat ...]

EXTEND Challenge the pupils to classify the different types of determiners, such as quantifiers [e.g. few; some], possessives [e.g. his] and so on.

PRACTISE

Pupil book page 7

APPLY

- When the pupils are writing factual reports or stating a point of view, encourage the use of determiners that help us generalise [e.g. some ...; most ...; many ...; a ...].
- Discuss the use of determiners when the pupils are writing lists of items [e.g. for instructions or when making plans in design and technology: 'I need: some ...; two ...'].
- When the pupils are writing a personal account such as a diary, discuss any determiners used [e.g. my; our; this].

ASSESS

Dictation: I sorted out <u>some</u> old clothes to put in <u>the</u> bag. Shall I put <u>these</u> books with <u>the</u> clothes?
Say: Underline all the determiners.

Pupil book answers

Determiners

Remember

A **determiner** is the word that comes before a **noun** or at the start of a **noun phrase**. The most common determiners are 'the' and 'a' or 'an', but other words can also be determiners.

the cat	a cat	that cat
my cat	some cats	this cat

Try it

1 Choose **determiners** from the box to complete each sentence. Use a different word each time.

> a an the some many every my our these this that those

I have ___some___ money in ___my___ pocket.

There are ___many___ fish in ___the___ sea.

I try to go for ___a___ walk ___every___ day.

I found ___those___ books in ___our___ attic.

___This___ car is much faster than ___that___ car.

Let's use ___these___ apples to make ___an___ apple pie.

2 Underline the **determiners** in each sentence. Then rewrite the sentence using different determiners.

Jenny left a bag at our house. _Jenny left her bag at his house._

The dog stole the burger. _That dog stole my burger._

Some people came to see the show. _Many people came to see our show._

Every athlete wants a gold medal. _That athlete wants the gold medal._

I found the money under a stone. _I found some money under this stone._

Sentence practice

Complete this sentence using at least two different **determiners**.

A black horse _ran down the street and jumped over our garden wall._

7

Accept alternative choices that make sense [e.g. these books; those apples]. If necessary, point out that 'an' cannot be used with 'apples' as it is a plural noun.

'This' should start with a capital letter as it is at the start of a sentence. The other determiners should begin with lower-case letters.

These are examples of suitable determiners. Other choices could be made. Compare the pupils' choices and how they affect the meaning of the sentence.

Determiners at the beginning of sentences should start with a capital letter.

This is just an example of a sentence using two determiners.

Lesson 5 Noun phrases 1

Focus building noun phrases using determiners, adjectives and other nouns

Key terms noun, noun phrase, determiner, adjective, adverb

Focus text In the forest clearing there stood three women. They were the oldest, frailest, thinnest women he had ever seen. They had crooked backs and withered, feeble arms. Their wrinkled skin hung from their ancient bones. They looked at him with sad watery eyes and spoke through cracked lips.

TEACH

Show the focus text and read it aloud. Discuss the mental image created of the women, referring to particular words and phrases [e.g. crooked backs; withered, feeble arms]. Ask the pupils what type of word is highlighted [nouns].

Remind the pupils that we often add words to a noun to describe it more clearly or specify it more exactly. Look at each noun in the focus text and underline the words that go with it [e.g. their wrinkled skin; sad watery eyes]. Recap that these are noun phrases [a group of words built around a noun].

Use examples from the focus text to discuss different types of word used in the noun phrases, such as:
- determiners – used before nouns or at the start of noun phrases to specify the noun [e.g. 'three women' tells us how many].
- adjectives – added to nouns to point out key features [e.g. feeble arms]. Explain that usually we use one or two adjectives with a noun, but here there is one noun phrase with a list of adjectives [the oldest, frailest, thinnest women]. Emphasise that this is done only occasionally for effect.
- nouns – sometimes used like adjectives to modify a noun [e.g. 'forest clearing' – both words are nouns but 'forest' is used to modify 'clearing'].

Invite the pupils to orally compose some more noun phrases to describe the women's hair or clothes, choosing adjectives carefully.

EXTEND Explain that we can add adverbs to adjectives [e.g. very thin; really ancient].

PRACTISE

Pupil book page 8

APPLY

- The pupils write interesting descriptions of characters or imaginary creatures, using carefully chosen adjectives in expanded noun phrases.
- The pupils write descriptions of settings, using noun phrases to give details about weather and atmosphere as well as describing what can be seen.
- Before the pupils write descriptions, remind them to note ideas for noun phrases. They should select words carefully, thinking about determiners and precise nouns as well as adjectives.
- When the pupils are revising writing, ask them to underline or highlight noun phrases that could be improved. Encourage the use of precise nouns and more adventurous adjectives.
- The pupils write sentences following patterns [e.g. starting with an adjective – 'grey shadows', 'thick smoke'; including a list of three adjectives for effect].

ASSESS

Dictation: A strange little man appeared before us. He had white hair and a very long grey beard.
Say: Underline the three noun phrases.

Pupil book answers

Noun phrases 1

Remember

Words can be added to a **noun** to give more detail about it. For example, you can add a **determiner**, **adjectives** or even another noun. This creates a longer **noun phrase**.

this forest   (determiner + noun)
tangled, dark forests   (adjective + adjective + noun)
the forest clearing   (determiner + noun + noun)

Try it

1 Underline the **noun phrase** that includes the **noun** shown in **bold**.

The gloomy forest **trees** closed over our heads.

My grandma always wears bright jangly **jewellery**.

Two shadowy **figures** stepped out of the doorway.

There was a large elaborate wedding **cake** in the shop window.

A swan has a long, slender **neck**.

Her yellow, curly **hair** was piled on top of her head.

2 Complete each noun phrase using **adjectives** to give more detail about the **noun** shown in **bold**.

On the doorstep, there stood two _____ scruffy little _____ **boys**.

They were the _dirtiest, scruffiest, filthiest_ **boys** you have ever seen.

They had _____ grimy _____ **faces** and _matted, unwashed_ **hair**.

They wore ____ grubby, threadbare ____ **coats** and _____ battered old _____ **shoes**.

One carried a _____ very shabby _____ **suitcase**.

Sentence practice

Write three sentences using **noun phrases** to describe a dragon.

The dragon had a scaly green body and a long spiny tail. He had red, glowing eyes and razor-sharp teeth. His long, flaming tongue kept flicking out of his gaping mouth.

8

Check that determiners are underlined as well as adjectives and nouns.

These are examples of adjectives that might be used to expand the nouns. Look for one or two appropriate adjectives – or perhaps three in one sentence for effect. Discuss the pupils' adjectives. Do they add relevant details? What effect is created? Have any been repeated? If so, is there an alternative?

Two adjectives before a noun are sometimes separated by a comma. At this stage, the pupils are not expected to use a comma between two adjectives. However, expect commas to be used between lists of three or more adjectives.

This is an example of how noun phrases might be used. You could ask the pupils to underline the noun phrases they have used. Do the adjectives add relevant details to the nouns? Which phrases are most effective?

Lesson 6 Noun phrases 2

Focus expanding noun phrases using a prepositional phrase after the noun

Key terms noun, noun phrase, preposition, prepositional phrase, adjective

Focus text He entered the ice palace through the doors of shimmering silver. Inside, great columns of white marble stretched to the sky. Snowflakes covered the floor beneath his feet. Light from hundreds of windows filled the room. Magnificent portraits in glittering frames hung from the walls.

TEACH

Show the focus text and read it aloud. Discuss the pupils' impressions of the palace [e.g. Ask: Is it real or imaginary? How do you feel about it?]. Encourage the pupils to refer to specific details in the text. Underline the noun phrases used to describe these features [e.g. the doors of shimmering silver, great columns of white marble, the floor beneath his feet].

Ask the pupils what they notice about these noun phrases. How do they add more detail about the noun? [e.g. some have adjectives, but they also have phrases added after the noun]

Explain that as well as adding adjectives before a noun, we can also add a phrase *after* the noun to give more detail about it. For example, in the phrase 'great columns of white marble', both the adjective before the noun and the phrase after it tell us more about the columns.

Look at other noun phrases in the focus text that include details added after the noun [e.g. doors of shimmering silver]. Explain that the words directly after the nouns are prepositions [of, beneath, from, in], so these are prepositional phrases. The pupils will be familiar with using prepositions to give more detail about the action in a sentence, but explain to them that when a prepositional phrase is added straight after a noun it is telling us more about the noun. It becomes part of the longer noun phrase.

Invite the pupils to orally construct some more noun phrases to describe an ice palace, using prepositions after the noun [e.g. a palace with shimmering towers; a glittering curtain of ice].

EXTEND Compare different ways of adding the same detail, discussing which ones sound better [e.g. a glittering, icy curtain/a glittering curtain of ice].

PRACTISE

Pupil book page 9

APPLY

- The pupils write descriptions of people and places [real or imagined] using prepositional phrases as well as adjectives to give more detail about nouns.
- When the pupils are writing descriptions, remind them to note and orally rehearse different ways of adding detail to nouns [e.g. silvery stars/stars of silver].
- When reading with the pupils, look for examples of expanded noun phrases with prepositions used to add detail after the noun. Record these and encourage the pupils to use them as models.
- The pupils describe objects or costumes using expanded noun phrases.

ASSESS

Dictation: He found an underground cave beneath the palace. It had smooth walls of white stone.
Say: Underline the longest possible noun phrase in each sentence.
Check: The whole noun phrase is underlined, including 'an' in the first phrase.

Pupil book answers

Noun phrases 2

Remember

As well as adding **adjectives** to a **noun**, you can also add a phrase starting with a **preposition** <u>after</u> the noun. This **prepositional phrase** adds more detail about the noun and becomes part of the **noun phrase**.

great columns <u>of white marble</u>

Try it

1 Underline the full **noun phrase** that includes the **noun** in **bold**.

He spoke to <u>the **animals** of the jungle</u>.

Did you see <u>the television **programme** about polar bears</u>?

<u>The elegant **lady** in the painting</u> was smiling at me.

<u>The history **book** from the library</u> was full of interesting facts.

<u>The **path** through the forest</u> led him to the waterfall.

I support <u>the best **team** in the world</u>.

2 Write a **noun phrase** with an **adjective** before the **noun** and a **prepositional phrase** after it.

the tree	the tall tree with the red leaves
the boat	the rusty fishing boat on the beach
the monster	the hideous monster with a terrible roar
the dog	the little dog with the injured leg
curtains	elegant curtains of red velvet
a painting	a famous painting by Van Gogh

Sentence practice

Write a sentence about a cottage. Use at least <u>two</u> longer **noun phrases**.

I saw a neat path of cobblestones leading to a pretty little cottage with a bright red door.

9

Check that the determiner 'the' is underlined as well as the prepositional phrase after the noun.

You could ask the pupils to circle the prepositions used in the noun phrases, as these might be useful in the activity below.

These are just examples of how the noun phrases might be expanded using adjectives and prepositional phrases.

Compare the pupils' answers, looking at which prepositions are used and what details are added.

This is just an example of a sentence showing noun phrases expanded with adjectives and prepositional phrases.

Lesson 7 Punctuating direct speech 1

Focus placing inverted commas and end punctuation in direct speech

Key terms direct speech, inverted commas, punctuation, comma, question mark, exclamation mark

Focus text "It's a spaceship" gasped Ruby.
"Do not be afraid" said a booming voice. "We come in peace"
"Did you hear that" asked Amit, grabbing Ruby's arm.

TEACH

Show the focus text. Ask the pupils how they can tell that it is an example of direct speech [e.g. inverted commas; clauses saying who is speaking; layout – new lines for new speakers]. Identify and underline the words spoken by the characters [the words inside the inverted commas].

Read the text aloud using appropriate expression. Discuss and add the missing punctuation marks at the end of the spoken words ['!' in the first sentence; comma and full stop in the second; '?' in the third].

Use the activity to remind the pupils that the punctuation mark goes *inside* the inverted commas – it belongs to the spoken words. When a reporting clause [e.g. gasped Ruby] follows, this punctuation mark is usually a comma, but a question mark or exclamation mark is used instead if appropriate. [Note: The pupils do not need to know the term 'reporting clause', but you can introduce it if you wish.]

Explain that in the second line of the focus text a character says two sentences. This means we can put the reporting clause *between* the two spoken sentences. To do this we use two sets of inverted commas. The first sentence follows the normal rules for punctuating direct speech, with a full stop after 'said a booming voice'. The second spoken sentence is placed inside another set of inverted commas. It starts with a capital letter and ends with a full stop [or '?'/'!' if required]. No new line is needed, as the speaker has not changed.

Invite the pupils to orally compose and write another example [e.g. "We have a message," boomed the voice. "Enter our spacecraft."].

EXTEND Explain that if we were to put the reporting clause in the *middle* of a spoken sentence, the reporting clause would be followed by a comma and the second part of the direct speech would begin with a lower-case letter.

PRACTISE

Pupil book page 10

APPLY

- The pupils write a line of direct speech to open or end a story [e.g. a question or exclamation].
- The pupils convert a comic-strip story into narrative using direct speech instead of speech bubbles.
- In pairs, the pupils act out or orally compose a short dialogue [e.g. a discovery; a quarrel; a wrong turn] and then write it as direct speech following the rules for sentence punctuation.
- The pupils write a conversation between two people in a story, using direct speech to develop character. Encourage the use of interesting speech verbs.

ASSESS

Dictation: "These are special stones," said the old man.
"How are they special?" asked the boy.
"Because they are magic," said the old man. "They will grant you three wishes."
Check: All sentences are correctly punctuated. There is a new line for each new speaker.

Pupil book answers

Punctuating direct speech 1

Remember

In **direct speech**, the spoken words and the **punctuation mark** at the end of them go inside the **inverted commas**. This punctuation mark is usually a **comma** but it can also be a **question mark** or **exclamation mark**.

"It's a spaceship!" gasped Ruby.

Sometimes a second spoken sentence, ending with a **full stop**, is added after 'said …'.

"Do not be afraid," said a booming voice. "We come in peace."

Try it

1 Add the missing **punctuation mark** at the end of the spoken words.

"What is that _?_ " asked Bella.

"It seems to be a stegosaurus _,_ " said Charlie thoughtfully.

"A stegosaurus _!_ " exclaimed Bella. "I thought they were extinct _._ "

"Well, this one clearly isn't _,_ " said Charlie.

"Watch out _!_ " shouted Bella. "It's coming this way _!_ "

2 Write each sentence with the correct **punctuation**.

What's that strange noise asked the woman.

  "What's that strange noise?" asked the woman.

Help screamed Jamie. The door is locked and I can't get out.

  "Help!" screamed Jamie. "The door is locked and I can't get out."

I'm so thirsty said the man. Please get me a drink of water.

  "I'm so thirsty," said the man. "Please get me a drink of water."

Sentence practice

Mum asks Jodie if she has fed the guinea pigs. Write their conversation as sentences of **direct speech**, using the correct **punctuation**.

  "Have you fed the guinea pigs yet?" asked Mum.

  "I'll do it in a minute," replied Jodie. "I just have to finish this."

10

You may wish to accept answers that use a comma instead of an exclamation mark, although the use of an exclamation mark is suggested by the verbs 'exclaimed' and 'shouted'.

Check the use of inverted commas, commas and other end punctuation, which should be *within* the inverted commas.

Also check the correct use of full stops and capital letters. There should be no capital letter at the start of the speech verbs [asked, screamed, said]. Full stops should mark the ends of sentences.

This is just an example of a suitable answer. Check all punctuation: inverted commas; commas or other end punctuation for the direct speech; full stops and capital letters; and apostrophes if used.

Lesson 8   Punctuating direct speech 2

Focus   punctuating direct speech where the reporting clause precedes the spoken words

Key terms   direct speech, inverted commas, comma

Focus text   "Where are you going?" asked the old lady.
The first man replied, "I am going to seek my fortune."
The second man answered, "I am going to seek adventure."
The third man said, "I am going to seek happiness."

TEACH

Show the focus text and read it aloud. Underline the words spoken in each sentence.

Discuss what is different about the presentation of the direct speech in the three replies [the part that tells us who is speaking comes before the spoken words].

Explain that in direct speech the reporting clause can be placed *before* the spoken words rather than after them. Use the focus text to look at the punctuation needed to do this. Explain that the spoken words are still inside the inverted commas and that we still use a comma to separate the reporting clause from the spoken words. But now the comma is placed after the reporting clause rather than after the spoken words. Circle the three commas after the speech verbs in the focus text.

Look at the spoken words inside the inverted commas in the three men's replies. Point out that each sentence is complete, with a capital letter at the start and full stop at the end *within* the inverted commas.

Ask the pupils to say the first sentence of the focus text, starting with the reporting clause [The old lady asked, "Where are you going?"]. Write the sentence, discussing the correct punctuation [comma after 'asked'; capital letter and question mark for the sentence within the inverted commas].

EXTEND   Ask the pupils to write their own rules and reminders for punctuating direct speech.

PRACTISE

Pupil book page 11

APPLY

- When the pupils are writing direct speech in stories, challenge them to include the reporting clause in different positions.
- Ask the pupils to revise a sample of direct speech, finding a place where the reporting clause could be moved to the start of the sentence or between two spoken sentences.
- The pupils use direct speech in a newspaper report, following the same rules for punctuation [e.g. The police officer said, "We will catch the thief."].
- The pupils rewrite part of a play script as direct speech. Compare these two ways of presenting speech [e.g. both use a new line for a new speaker; direct speech uses inverted commas and reporting clauses].
- Make it a proofreading target for the pupils to check that direct speech is correctly punctuated.

ASSESS

Dictation: "What's that you have there?" asked the elf.
The wizard said, "It's a new invention of mine."
"What does it do?" asked the elf.
The wizard smiled and said, "Let me show you."

Check: All sentences are correctly punctuated, including the use of an apostrophe in the contractions.

Pupil book answers

Punctuating direct speech 2

Remember

Sometimes in **direct speech**, the sentence begins with the part that tells you who is speaking. A **comma** is used to separate this part of the sentence from the spoken words. The spoken words still go inside the **inverted commas**, complete with their own **punctuation**.

The first man replied, "I am going to seek my fortune."

Try it

1 Rewrite each sentence so that it starts with the part telling us who is speaking. Use the correct **punctuation**.

"Look out!" someone shouted.

Someone shouted, "Look out!"

"You are a very wise man," the chief said.

The chief said, "You are a very wise man."

"Has anyone seen my bag?" Erin asked her friends.

Erin asked her friends, "Has anyone seen my bag?"

These are just examples of what might be said. Accept any plausible sentence.

Check that a comma has been added after the given reporting clause. Then check that a correctly punctuated sentence has been included inside inverted commas. The final punctuation mark [full stop, '!' or '?'] depends on the sentence, but it should be *within* the inverted commas.

2 Complete each sentence by adding what is said. Use the correct **punctuation**.

The teacher announced , "Today we are going to the art gallery."

The boy shrieked , "It's a ghost!"

The doctor asked , "Do you feel dizzy?"

The pirate roared , "Tell me where to find the treasure!"

With a smile, the wolf said , "Let me show you the way."

Sentence practice

Archie asks Mo if he wants to play. Write Archie's question and Mo's reply as **direct speech**.

Archie asks, "Do you want to play football?"

"That would be great," replies Mo.

11

This is just an example. The wording may not be exactly the same.

The reporting clause is given for the first sentence to ensure that one sentence, at least, begins with the reporting clause. Check the punctuation of both the question and the reply.

Lesson 9 Pronouns within sentences

Focus   using pronouns within sentences to avoid repetition; linking nouns to pronouns

Key terms   noun, pronoun, noun phrase, proper noun, **personal pronoun**, determiner

Focus text   As the ball hit the window, Adam heard it smash. Adam knew he was in trouble.
Mrs Kemp saw Adam from her office window and she was angry with him.
Mrs Kemp pointed at the ball and shouted, "Bring that to me."

TEACH

Show the focus text and read it aloud. Discuss the events and who the characters are.

Ask what type of word is highlighted [pronouns – they replace a noun or proper noun/name]. Read each sentence and identify the noun or noun phrase that the pronoun replaces. Ask: What does 'it' refer to? [the window] Who is 'he'/'him'? [Adam] Who is 'she'/'me'? [Mrs Kemp] What does 'that' refer to? [the ball] Write the relevant noun or noun phrase above each pronoun. Discuss how we know what they refer to [e.g. because the noun has already been mentioned in the sentence].

Read the sentences as they would sound with all the nouns in place [e.g. Adam knew Adam was in trouble.]. Discuss why it sounds better with pronouns [e.g. there is less repetition; it is clearer].

Remind the pupils that pronouns are words that stand in place of nouns, proper nouns and noun phrases. We use pronouns to avoid repeating the same noun or noun phrase within a sentence. Introduce the term 'personal pronoun' and discuss other personal pronouns. Ask: What if there were two children in the focus text? [they, them – plural pronouns] What if you broke the window? [I, me] What if it were Annie, not Adam? [she, her]

Point out that determiners are also sometimes used as pronouns. For example, in the last sentence, 'that' is a pronoun because it is used *in place of* the noun 'ball'. However, it would be a determiner if still followed by the noun [e.g. Bring that ball to me.].

Explain that, in the focus text, the word 'her' is not highlighted, although 'her' can be a pronoun [e.g. Mrs Kemp appeared and Adam saw her.]. This is because the word 'her' here replaces a possessive noun [Mrs Kemp's] and is followed by a noun phrase [office window] so it is being used as a possessive determiner rather than a pronoun. [Note: Possessives will be covered again in Lesson 21.]

EXTEND   Explore other determiners that can be used as pronouns [e.g. this; these; some].

PRACTISE

Pupil book page 12

APPLY

- The pupils write stories or accounts in the first and third person, using pronouns to avoid repetition.
- Encourage the pupils to look at the use of pronouns in different types of text [e.g. 'you' in persuasive texts]. Discuss who they refer to in each case.
- When the pupils are rehearsing and editing longer sentences, encourage them to check whether they would sound better using pronouns rather than repeating nouns.

ASSESS

Dictation: The team deserved to win the cup and they proudly showed it to the cheering crowd.
Say: Underline the pronouns in this sentence.

Pupil book answers

Pronouns within sentences

Remember

A **pronoun** is used in place of a **noun**, a **proper noun** or a **noun phrase**. For example, you can use **personal pronouns** (e.g. he, she, it, they) to avoid repeating the same name or noun within a sentence.

As the ball hit <u>the window</u>, Alfie heard <u>it</u> smash.
<u>Alfie</u> knew <u>he</u> was in trouble.

Try it

1 Complete each sentence by adding a suitable **pronoun**.

The princess asked the wizard to help ___her___ .

The girl took the box into the garden and buried ___it___ .

I made a puppet from the sock that Mum gave ___me___ .

As Nathan and I marched by, people came to cheer ___us___ .

I heard you were ill so I made this card for ___you___ .

I read the instructions but I couldn't understand ___them___ .

2 Rewrite each sentence using at least <u>two</u> **pronouns** in place of some of the nouns and proper nouns.

Soraya and I saw the twins but the twins did not see Soraya and me.
 Soraya and I saw the twins but they did not see us.

Gran and Granddad hoped Amy would visit Gran and Granddad but Amy was too busy.
 Gran and Granddad hoped Amy would visit them but she was too busy.

Jason found the bike in the wood but Jason did not know that the bike was stolen.
 Jason found the bike in the wood but he did not know that it was stolen.

Sentence practice

Write a sentence about finding some treasure, including the **pronouns** 'they' and 'it'. Make sure it is clear who or what the pronouns refer to.
 The children found a pot of gold and they took it home.

12

In this activity, the pronoun should match the person and number used in the sentence [e.g. the princess/her; the instructions/them].

Accept other pronouns if they make sense [e.g. As Nathan and I marched by, people came to cheer him/ me.].

At least two of the nouns or proper nouns in each sentence should have been replaced with pronouns to avoid repetition.

The pupils might replace all the nouns and noun phrases with pronouns. You may wish to discuss whether this makes the sentence unclear [e.g. He found it in there but he did not know that it was stolen.].

[Note: The clear use of pronouns will be covered in Lesson 22].

This is an example of a single sentence that uses the given pronouns to avoid repeating nouns or noun phrases. The reference of the pronouns should be clear because of the nouns used by the pupils in the first part of the sentence.

Lesson 10 Pronouns across sentences

Focus using pronouns across sentences to avoid repetition and create links [cohesion]

Key terms pronoun, noun, personal pronoun, paragraph

Focus text The pupils from Class 4 will be visiting the Space Centre on Monday. I am sure they will enjoy the many activities it has to offer. This is an important opportunity for them to learn more about the Earth and space.

TEACH

Show the focus text. Read it aloud. Discuss what type of text it is [school newsletter sent to parents].

Ask the pupils what type of word is highlighted [pronouns – 'I', 'they', 'it', 'them' are personal pronouns; 'this' is often a determiner but here is used as a pronoun]. Read the text and discuss who or what each pronoun refers to ['I' – head teacher; 'they'/'them'– the pupils from Class 4; it – the Space Centre; 'This' – the visit]. Discuss how we know this [by reading the previous sentence]. Show the links across sentences by using different colours to underline the nouns and their linked pronouns.

Discuss why the pronouns have been used [e.g. to avoid repeating phrases such as 'the pupils', as this repetition can sound clumsy]. Explain that the focus text shows how we can use pronouns across more than one sentence. Here the pronouns link back to ideas in the previous sentences. As well as avoiding repetition, using pronouns also helps to link sentences together.

Explain that when we do this, it must be clear who or what the pronoun refers to. If we use a pronoun too many times in a paragraph, the reader might forget who it refers to. So sometimes we need to repeat the noun or use a 'synonymous' noun. For example, in the last sentence of the focus text we could use 'the children' rather than 'them' or 'the pupils'.

Invite the pupils to orally compose another sentence for the letter, deciding whether to use pronouns or nouns.

EXTEND Discuss the idea of ambiguity, when the meaning of a pronoun is unclear. Say the sentence 'The pupils discussed ideas with the staff. They were impressed.' Ask: Who was impressed? The pupils or the staff? [Note: Ambiguous pronouns are covered in more detail in **Grammar 5**.]

PRACTISE

Pupil book page 13

APPLY

- The pupils write diary entries, focusing on the use of personal pronouns within and between sentences. Encourage them to think about when to use nouns and when to use pronouns.
- Remind the pupils to regularly reread paragraphs to check their use of pronouns. Are names or nouns repeated too many times? Are there too many pronouns? Is it clear what each pronoun stands for?
- When the pupils are writing explanations, demonstrate using the word 'this' as a pronoun to refer back to something mentioned in the previous sentence [e.g. This leads to ...; This causes ...].
- The pupils write a story with two characters of the same sex. Discuss when it is necessary to use the name so that the reader is clear who 'she'/'her'/'hers' or 'he'/'him'/'his' refers to.

ASSESS

Dictation: Rosie looked at baby Oscar. She smiled at him and he gurgled back at her.
Say: Underline the pronouns in the second sentence. Is it clear who they refer to? Explain why or why not.
Answer: Yes, because Rosie is female and Oscar is male, so the pronouns can only refer to one of them.

Pupil book answers

Pronouns across sentences

Remember

Pronouns can also be used to help link sentences together. However, it must be clear who or what each pronoun refers to.

The children from Class 4 will be visiting the Space Centre on Monday. I am sure they will enjoy the many activities it has to offer.

Try it

1 Read both sentences. Circle the **noun** or the **noun phrase** that each underlined pronoun refers to.

(Nina) saw the cat with the red collar. She phoned the owner at once.

(The virus) has spread to every computer in the world. We cannot stop it.

The giant gently carried (the little boy) inside. He placed him on the table.

The boys went to see (the chimpanzees.) They were kept in a large enclosure.

We enjoyed (a tasty breakfast.) This consisted of eggs, toast, yoghurt and fruit juice.

2 Rewrite the second sentence each time, using **pronouns**.

The footballers spoke to Yusuf. Yusuf said that he would meet the footballers the next day.

He said that he would meet them the next day.

Aisha searched for her friends. When Aisha found her friends, Aisha told her friends what Aisha had done.

When she found them, she told them what she had done.

Harry gave the book to Leo and Jake. Leo and Jake lost the book but Leo and Jake did not tell Harry.

They lost it but they did not tell him.

Sentence practice

Write two sentences about Alice and her brother. Use **pronouns** in the second sentence.

Alice took her little brother to the park. He told her he wanted to play on the swings.

13

Discuss with the pupils how they knew what each pronoun refers to, tracing the link back to the nouns and noun phrases in the previous sentence.

Discuss how the context also helps [e.g. it must be the giant placing the little boy on the table – it would not make sense the other way round].

Read out the first sentence and the new version of the second sentence. Discuss with the pupils whether the meaning of each pronoun is clear in the new sentences.

This is just an example of a suitable set of sentences.

Revision 1 answers

This page revises punctuation introduced in earlier books. The punctuation on this page should now be secure in the pupils' writing. If not, these areas should be addressed immediately.

The focus of each activity is given to help identify areas that need reinforcement.

Revision 1

Focus: demarcating sentence boundaries

1 Add the missing **full stop** and **capital letters** in the sentences below.

I was hoping to visit my friend Jamila in Manchester during August. I know Connor wants to come with me so he can visit old Trafford.

Focus: commas in lists

There should be no comma before 'and'.

2 Rewrite each sentence, using **commas** correctly.

Chimney pots rattled doors slammed and windows shook.
Chimney pots rattled, doors slammed and windows shook.

We need fresh berries skimmed milk and a tub of ice cream.
We need fresh berries, skimmed milk and a tub of ice cream.

The creature had three eyes four large ears and a huge mouth.
The creature had three eyes, four large ears and a huge mouth.

On sports day we had an obstacle course an egg and spoon race and a dancing competition.
On sports day we had an obstacle course, an egg and spoon race and a dancing competition.

Focus: apostrophes to mark contracted forms

Accept other contractions that make sense [e.g.'we've'/'Dad's' rather than 'you've']. The contractions must be spelt correctly with the apostrophe correctly placed.

Contractions like these are often used in direct speech, so the pupils should check that they use them correctly when proofreading their work.

3 Complete the sentence below using a **contraction** that makes sense.

"I knew you   wouldn't   understand," the girl grumbled.

"I can't believe what   you've   done!" Mum said.

"We must hurry or   we'll   be late," said Dad.

"Why don't you look where   you're   going?" snapped Toby.

"   It's   the last day of term today!' squealed Priti.

4 Add the **punctuation mark** needed at the end of each sentence.

Anoushka said my singing was no good .

What a cheek !

I didn't know what to say .

Is my voice that bad ?

Tell me the truth .

Focus: demarcating the end of sentences with full stops, question marks, exclamation marks

If necessary, remind the pupils that exclamations usually start with 'What' or 'How'.

14

The emphasis on this page is on work on words and word structure covered in **Grammar 3**. Word structure has not yet been covered in this book, so it is important to check that the pupils have retained this knowledge.

The focus of each activity is given to help you identify areas where the pupils might need further revision.

5 Draw a line to match each **prefix** to the correct word to make a new word.

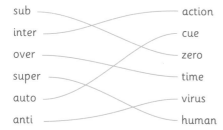

sub	action
inter	cue
over	zero
super	time
auto	virus
anti	human

Focus: forming words using a range of prefixes [e.g. super–; anti–; auto–]

Discuss the meaning of the prefixes and the new words formed.

6 Rewrite each sentence using the correct form of the **determiner**.

Zara told me a amusing story.
 Zara told me an amusing story.

They discovered a underground cave.
 They discovered an underground cave.

There was a icy wind blowing outside.
 There was an icy wind blowing outside.

I found a odd sock with an hole in it.
 I found an odd sock with a hole in it.

Focus: use of 'a' or 'an' according to whether the next word begins with a consonant or a vowel sound

Check that both words are corrected in the fourth sentence.

7 Add a **suffix** to complete the **noun** in **bold**.

We took a **measure** ment of the rainfall.

I was surprised by the **mild** ness of the weather.

Uncle Antoni told us about the **form** ation of fossils.

The captain showed good **leader** ship skills.

He wrote a **greet** ing in the card.

Focus: forming nouns using suffixes [e.g. –ness; –er; –ment]

The suffixes must be spelt correctly.

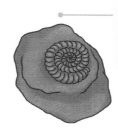

8 Complete each sentence with a **longer noun phrase**.

On the flower, there was a beautiful butterfly with red and blue wings.

At the library, he chose a fascinating book about robots.

For a special treat, they bought a box of delicious cakes filled with jam.

Focus: expanded noun phrases to describe or specify

15

Look for noun phrases expanded by the addition of modifying adjectives and/or nouns and prepositional phrases. These are just examples.

Compare the pupils' answers, discussing which are most descriptive, specific or interesting.

Writing task 1: Analysis sheet

Tick the circles to show amount of evidence found in writing:
1 No evidence
2 Some evidence
3 Clear evidence

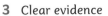

Pupil name: _____

Date: _____

Assessing punctuation

The writing sample demonstrates:	Evidence		
sentence boundaries demarcated with capital letters and full stops.	①	②	③
question marks and exclamation marks used appropriately when required.	①	②	③
capital letters used for 'I' and proper nouns.	①	②	③
commas used to separate items in a list [e.g. It had short legs, a huge body and a long tail.].	①	②	③
apostrophes used in contracted forms [e.g. it wasn't] or for singular possession [e.g. dragon's tail].	①	②	③
inverted commas and other punctuation marks used to indicate direct speech [e.g. I shouted, "Go away!"].	①	②	③

Assessing grammar and sentence structure

The writing sample demonstrates:	Evidence		
grammatically correct sentences [e.g. noun–verb or pronoun–verb agreement].	①	②	③
a variety of sentence types [e.g. exclamations and questions – 'What a surprise!'; 'Do you believe me?'].	①	②	③
sentences with more than one clause.	①	②	③
a range of subordinating conjunctions to expand ideas [e.g. while; since; although].	①	②	③
a consistent use of past tense, including perfect forms [e.g. I have not told anyone else.].	①	②	③
the use of pronouns to avoid repetition and make links.	①	②	③
expanded noun phrases to describe, specify and add detail [e.g. a green body with pointed scales].	①	②	③

Key target: _____

Writing task 1: Pupil checklist

Name: _Aishani_ Date: _18.09.20_

Reread what you have written to check that it makes sense. Tick the circle if you have correctly used the punctuation or grammar feature in your writing.

Punctuation

☑ I have used capital letters and full stops to punctuate sentences.

☑ I have used question marks or exclamation marks where needed.

☑ I have used capital letters for 'I' and any names.

☑ I have used commas to separate items in a list.

☑ I have used apostrophes in contracted forms (e.g. it wasn't) and for possession (e.g. dragon's tail).

☑ I have used inverted commas and other punctuation in direct speech (e.g. I shouted, "Go away!").

Grammar and sentences

☑ I have written in sentences and checked that they make sense, for example by checking verbs and nouns.

☑ I have used different sentence types (e.g. an exclamation to show surprise).

◯ I have used sentences with more than one clause.

◯ I have used different conjunctions to develop ideas in sentences, for example to show time or give reasons.

☑ I have used the past tense to write about what happened.

☑ I have used pronouns rather than repeating nouns.

◯ I have used longer noun phrases to describe and give details (e.g. a large, lumbering creature with a long neck).

Teacher feedback

My key target: _____

_____

Lesson 11 Adverbials

Focus introducing the term 'adverbial'; identifying adverbials [words and phrases] in sentences

Key terms adverb, preposition, phrase, **adverbial**

Focus text <u>Carefully</u> chop each beetroot <u>into bite-size pieces</u>.
<u>Then</u> mix the ingredients <u>together</u> <u>in a large bowl</u>.
Boil <u>gently</u> <u>for about 15 minutes</u>.
Keep stirring <u>all the time</u>.

TEACH

Show the focus text. Discuss what type of text it is taken from [e.g. instructions; recipe]. Read each sentence and discuss the purpose of the underlined words and phrases. Establish that they add extra detail to the main instruction [e.g. *how* to chop each beetroot; *when* and *where* to mix the ingredients; *how/how long* to boil the mixture]. Ask the pupils what kind of words and phrases are underlined [adverbs – e.g. 'carefully'; phrases starting with prepositions – e.g. 'into bite-size pieces'].

Introduce the term 'adverbial'. Explain that this term is used for any word [adverb], phrase or clause that tells us more about the verb or the main action in the sentence – so all the underlined phrases in the focus text are adverbials because they tell us more about how, where, when the actions should be performed. [Note: Subordinate clauses can also be adverbials – e.g. Stir <u>until it is ready</u>. This is covered in more detail in Lesson 14.]

Explain that sentences can contain more than one adverbial, adding different details about the actions. As shown in the focus text, these adverbials can be placed in different positions in a sentence; for example, the pupils will be familiar with using time adverbials at the start of sentences. [Note: 'Fronting' different adverbials is the focus of the next lesson, Lesson 12.]

Invite the pupils to orally compose more recipe instructions, using adverbials to add detail to verbs or actions [e.g. Drain the vegetables ...; Pour the mixture ...; Serve ...].

EXTEND Challenge the pupils to experiment with reordering sentences, moving adverbials to different positions [e.g. Chop each beetroot <u>carefully</u> <u>into bite-size pieces</u>. <u>Gently</u> boil <u>for about 15 minutes</u>.].

PRACTISE

Pupil book page 18

APPLY

- Encourage the pupils to look at how adverbials are used in different types of text [e.g. explanations; descriptions].
- When reading with the pupils, collect examples of sentences with adverbials used in different positions. Encourage the pupils to look out for further examples in their independent reading.
- When the pupils are writing, remind them to orally compose sentences, adding adverbials to give more detail about how, when and where.
- When the pupils are writing stories, encourage the use of adverbials to change the scene or move the story on [e.g. in the morning; on the other side of the river].

ASSESS

Dictation: She was standing (in the middle of a field) (at midnight) (with snowflakes in her hair).
Say: Circle the three adverbials in this sentence.

Pupil book answers

Adverbials

Remember

Adverbials are words, phrases or clauses that add more detail about the **verb** or event in a sentence. For example, they can say where, when or how an action is performed. An adverbial can be a single **adverb** or a **phrase** that works like an adverb.

Carefully, chop each beetroot into bite-size pieces.

Try it

1 Underline the **adverbials** in these sentences.

At daybreak, a ship appeared through the sea mist.

He quickly read the letter by the light of a candle.

She travelled for many days without a rest.

We sometimes go kayaking at the weekend.

Suddenly, there was a glimpse of sunlight between the clouds.

In the morning, the king arrived to a fanfare of trumpets.

2 Add **adverbials** in the spaces to complete these sentences.

After a long while, the man sat down with a sigh.

Pour the mixture carefully into small bowls.

I always have cereal for breakfast.

She soon started shouting loudly.

I haven't seen Georgia at school since Tuesday.

Suddenly, we heard a strange noise from outside.

Sentence practice

Write a sentence using the verb 'hobbled' and two **adverbials**.

The boy hobbled painfully towards the chair.

18

This activity helps to reinforce that adverbials can be used in different positions in the sentence. You could discuss this with the pupils.

Point out that the rest of the sentence makes sense without the adverbials: it is a main clause.

These are just examples of adverbials that make sense in the context. Compare the pupils' answers. Look for adverbials that give details about where, when, how or how long. Look for single adverbs, phrases or clauses.

Adverbials at the start of sentences should begin with capital letters.

This is just an example of a sentence with two adverbials – an adverb and a prepositional phrase.

If the pupils have started the sentence with an adverbial, there should be a comma after it. This is the focus of the next two lessons, but you could point this out now.

Lesson 12 Fronted adverbials

Focus using fronted adverbials in sentences

Key terms adverbial, **fronted adverbial**, adverb, phrase

Focus text <u>In a little village</u>, <u>on the edge of a wood</u>, there lived an old man. <u>Early one morning</u>, there was a knock <u>at the old man's door</u>. "Who can that be?" the old man grumbled <u>to himself</u>. <u>Slowly</u>, he shuffled <u>towards the door</u>.

TEACH

Show the focus text and read it aloud. Discuss the underlined phrases. Ask: What is their purpose? What are they called? [e.g. they give extra information about the event in a sentence; adverbials] Discuss what each adverbial adds to the sentence [details about where, when, how].

Ask the pupils what they notice about the position of the adverbials in the sentences [e.g. there are adverbials at the start of sentences as well as at the end].

Explain that adverbials can be added at the start [or front] of the sentence. An adverbial in this position is called a fronted adverbial. We can start sentences with adverbials that say where [In a little village], when [Early one morning] or how [Slowly]. Fronted adverbials can be used to clearly signal information [e.g. when or where an event takes place], to draw attention to how an action is performed [e.g. to show character or feelings] and to vary sentence openings.

[Note: If you wish, you can explain at this point that a comma is used after a fronted adverbial, as shown in the focus text. This will be the focus of the next lesson, Lesson 13.]

Say some sentences with adverbials and ask the pupils to repeat each sentence with the adverbial fronted [e.g. The old man opened the door cautiously. There was a box on the doorstep.].

EXTEND Explain that not all adverbials can be fronted [e.g. 'To himself, the old man grumbled.' sounds odd]. Discuss other examples where sentences cannot be reordered.

PRACTISE

Pupil book page 19

APPLY

- The pupils write stories, accounts and newspaper reports, using fronted adverbials to indicate time and place [e.g. Within minutes; Before long; Towards nightfall; Through the tunnel; At the end of the lane].
- The pupils use fronted adverbials to show the feelings of story characters [e.g. Angrily; Reluctantly].
- The pupils write poems, starting each line with an adverbial [e.g. Suddenly; Quickly; Through the door].
- When the pupils are writing stories, discuss the use of fronted adverbials to add drama at an exciting point in the story [e.g. Without warning; In a flash; Instantly; Within seconds; Only metres away].
- Encourage the pupils to look for fronted adverbials in other types of text, and to collect examples to use in their own writing [e.g. in instructions – Once cool; in descriptions – In the bedroom; in reports – Usually, Sometimes].
- Set the pupils the target of varying sentence openings [e.g. using an adverb to say how, a prepositional phrase to say where or when].

ASSESS

Dictation: <u>Quietly</u>, the thief opened the door. <u>In the middle of the room</u>, there was a table.
Say: Underline the fronted adverbials.

Pupil book answers

Fronted adverbials

Remember

Sometimes an **adverbial** is placed at the start (or <u>front</u>) of the sentence. This is called a **fronted adverbial**.

<u>In a little village</u>, there lived an old man.
<u>Early one morning</u>, there was a knock at the door.
<u>Slowly</u>, the old man shuffled towards the door.

Try it

1 Tick the sentences that start with a **fronted adverbial**.

Quickly, Dad prepared the meal. ✓

They saw a ship far away on the horizon. ☐

At the museum, we saw a dinosaur skeleton. ✓

She stormed angrily out of the room. ☐

Within minutes, the police arrived. ✓

In the silent room, a baby was sleeping. ✓

2 Complete each sentence by adding a **fronted adverbial** to say when, where or how.

<u>Towards the end of the day</u>, a farmer was walking home from his fields.

<u>At the end of a lane</u>, I saw a badger.

<u>Shortly before midnight</u>, a light appeared in the distance.

<u>Suddenly</u>, we heard footsteps.

<u>Happily</u>, the children played on the beach.

These are just examples of possible fronted adverbials. Look for the use of both adverbs and prepositional phrases to say where, when or how. Compare the pupils' answers.

Check that the fronted adverbials start with capital letters.

Sentence practice

Write <u>three</u> sentences about snow falling. Start with these **fronted adverbials**.

During the night, <u>snow began to fall.</u>

Outside, <u>the sky was a cold, bleak grey.</u>

Silently, <u>soft snowflakes landed on the fields and trees.</u>

19

These are just examples of possible sentences beginning with the fronted adverbials.

Lesson 13 Commas after fronted adverbials

Focus using commas after fronted adverbials

Key terms fronted adverbial, comma, adverb, phrase, preposition

Focus text Immediately after dinner, she went to the study. Cautiously, she took the box from the drawer. Really slowly, she lifted the lid. In the box, she found the ring.

TEACH

Show the focus text and read it aloud. Discuss what we can deduce about the character's actions from clues in the text. Ask the pupils to identify the fronted adverbial in each sentence, discussing how these help to show feelings and build tension. For example, ask: What does 'cautiously' suggest? Underline the fronted adverbials [Immediately after dinner, Cautiously, Really slowly, In the bottom of the box].

Ask the pupils what punctuation mark is used after each fronted adverbial [comma]. Read the focus text again so that the pupils can hear how this is reflected in speech with a slight pause after the fronted adverbial. Ask the pupils to use a curled finger to represent the comma as you say the sentence.

Remind the pupils that commas are used to clearly show the breaks between different parts of a sentence. Explain that when we put an adverbial at the start or front of a sentence, the comma after it clearly separates it from the main sentence. The fronted adverbial might be a single adverb [e.g. Cautiously, …] a phrase starting with a preposition [e.g. In the bottom of the box, …] or sometimes a combination of these.

Some adverbials consist of more than one adverb, or of an adverb that adds meaning to a phrase [e.g. Really slowly, …; Immediately after dinner, …]. The comma comes after the complete phrase, separating it from the main clause.

Say some more sentences using different types of adverbial [e.g. She carefully removed the ring. The door opened at that very moment. She left the room very quietly.]. Invite the pupils to say the sentences with the adverbial at the start, using a curled finger to show where the comma is needed [e.g. Carefully, she removed the ring. At that very moment, the door opened. Very quietly, she left the room.].

EXTEND Explain that if a sentence starts with two separate adverbials, we put a comma after each one [e.g. In the bottom of the box, right in the corner, she saw the ring.].

PRACTISE

Pupil book page 20

APPLY

- The pupils use sentences like those in the focus text as models for writing new sentences, automatically adding the comma after the fronted adverbial.
- When the pupils are rehearsing sentences orally, remind them to use a curled finger to show where the comma is needed.
- The pupils write descriptive sentences or poems beginning with repeated adverbials to practise the use of commas after fronted adverbials [e.g. Through the magic window, …].
- Make it a proofreading target for the pupils to check that commas are used after fronted adverbials.

ASSESS

Dictation: At midnight, the church bells began to ring. All over the kingdom, people rushed into the streets. Everywhere, people were cheering and dancing in the moonlight.
Check: All fronted adverbials are followed by commas.

Pupil book answers

Commas after fronted adverbials

Remember

When an **adverbial** is placed at the start or front of a sentence, a **comma** is used to clearly separate the adverbial from the main sentence.

<u>Immediately after dinner</u>, she went to the study.
<u>Cautiously</u>, she took the box from the drawer.
<u>In the box</u>, she found the ring.

Try it

1 Complete each sentence by adding a **comma** after the **fronted adverbial**.

From somewhere in the distance, a voice was singing.

Without warning, there was a sudden rush of water.

Just a few metres above them, there was a spaceship.

Later that night, the wizards gathered for a meeting.

Shortly after the war, William started a new business.

With great enthusiasm, the children set to work building a den.

2 Rewrite each sentence so that it begins with the **adverbial**. Punctuate it correctly.

She watched and waited anxiously. Anxiously, she watched and waited.

The lion paused for a moment. For a moment, the lion paused.

They made their way home wearily. Wearily, they made their way home.

We warmed up before the game. Before the game, we warmed up.

He closed the door without a word. Without a word, he closed the door.

Sentence practice

Write <u>two</u> sentences about a stormy night. Start each sentence with a fronted adverbial.

On a dark and stormy night, a man was travelling home. In the

distance, he heard a rumble of thunder.

20

If the pupils have difficulty with this, ask them to first identify the main clause – the part that makes sense by itself – and then to underline the extra phrase added at the start of the sentence. The comma should then separate the two parts of the sentence.

Ask the pupils to read the sentences aloud so they can hear the effect of moving the adverbial and adding the comma.

The sentences should begin with capital letters and end with full stops, as well as having commas after the fronted adverbial.

These are just examples of sentences starting with suitable adverbials. Check that both sentences begin with a capital letter and end with a full stop as well as having commas after the fronted adverbial.

Lesson 14 Fronting subordinate clauses

Focus moving subordinate clauses to the front of sentences; using a comma after a fronted clause

Key terms clause, conjunction, main clause, subordinate clause, adverbial, comma

Focus text The shop was closed.
When he arrived, the shop was closed.
Although it was nine o'clock, the shop was closed.
Because it was flooded, the shop was closed.

TEACH

Show the first sentence of the focus text. Invite the pupils to add a subordinate clause giving more detail about the event described in the main clause [e.g. The shop was closed when/while/because ...].

Show the second sentence. Ask the pupils to identify the subordinate clause. Remind the pupils that the subordinate clause begins with a conjunction and adds more detail to the main clause [e.g. saying when the shop was closed]. Underline the subordinate clause [When he arrived]. Repeat with the other two sentences, underlining the subordinate clauses and discussing what they add to the main clause [e.g. contrast – 'Although ...'; reason – 'Because ...'].

Discuss what the pupils notice about the subordinate clauses in these three sentences [e.g. they are at the beginning of the sentences; they are followed by a comma].

Remind the pupils that we use subordinate clauses starting with conjunctions to give more detail about the event in the main clause – for example, saying why, when or how an event happened. Explain that these subordinate clauses can function as adverbials because they add information to the main clause. Just like other adverbials, subordinate clauses can be moved and placed at the beginning of a sentence. This draws attention to the information given in the subordinate clause.

Explain that when a subordinate clause is placed at the beginning or front of a sentence, it is separated from the main clause by a comma. Ask the pupils to orally construct other sentences starting with conjunctions [e.g. While ...; As ...], using a curled finger to represent the comma.

EXTEND Invite the pupils to construct sentences starting with subordinate clauses using a wider range of conjunctions [e.g. Even though ...; Once ...].

PRACTISE

Pupil book page 21

APPLY

- When the pupils are writing stories, encourage them to start sentences with conjunctions [e.g. When; While; As] and to orally rehearse the sentences before writing them down.
- The pupils compose sentences starting with conjunctions such as 'While' or 'Although' to change the focus of a story [e.g. While Joe was celebrating, Jake was ...].
- Encourage the pupils to look for sentences starting with conjunctions in non-fiction texts [e.g. explanations – When, As, Because; instructions – Before it sets ...; reports – Although].
- The pupils revise a story, looking for an opportunity to move or add a subordinate clause to the start of a sentence. They then rehearse sentences orally to hear the effect of the change.

ASSESS

Dictation: Before you begin, make sure you warm up properly. If you are cold, try running on the spot.
Say: Underline the subordinate clauses.
Check: Both subordinate clauses are followed by commas.

Pupil book answers

Fronting subordinate clauses

Remember

Subordinate clauses starting with **conjunctions** give more detail about the **main clause**. When a subordinate clause is placed at the start of a sentence, it is separated from the main clause by a **comma**.

<u>Although it was nine o'clock</u>, the shop was closed.

<u>Because it was flooded</u>, the shop was closed.

Try it

1 Rewrite each sentence with the **subordinate clause** at the beginning of the sentence. Punctuate the sentence correctly.

The wind grew stronger as the sky grew darker.

 As the sky grew darker, the wind grew stronger.

She had never been to the castle even though she lived nearby.

 Even though she lived nearby, she had never been to the castle.

He did not answer his phone because it was late.

 Because it was late, he did not answer his phone.

2 Complete the **subordinate clause** at the start of each sentence. Punctuate it correctly.

 <u>While</u> they were sleeping,   Maggie was busy in the garden.

 <u>As</u> we clambered up the cliffs,   we could see for miles.

 <u>When</u> they got there,   they found that the cave was empty.

 <u>If</u> you press the red button,   the rocket will be launched.

 <u>Although</u> he tried hard,   he never did solve the puzzle.

Sentence practice

Write <u>two</u> sentences. Start one sentence with the **conjunction** 'as' and one with 'when'.

 As the goblin came closer, Luke could see that he was angry.

 When he spoke, his voice was full of fury.

21

Check that the sentences are correctly punctuated with a capital letter and full stop and a comma after the fronted subordinate clause.

If necessary, ask the pupils to first underline the subordinate clause. Remind them that it starts with a conjunction and adds detail to the main clause – the sentence part that makes sense on its own.

These are just examples of suitable subordinate clauses starting with the given conjunction. Encourage the pupils to orally compose sentences before writing them to check the sense and effect. Compare the pupils' answers.

A comma should be added after each subordinate clause.

These are just examples of sentences starting with the conjunctions. Invite the pupils to read their sentences aloud to discuss the effect.

Check that the sentences are correctly punctuated with a comma after the fronted subordinate clause.

Lesson 15 Singular and plural nouns

Focus regular and irregular plural nouns; singular and plural determiners

Key terms noun, singular, plural, determiner, **irregular plural**, **collective noun**

Focus text A lone wolf chased an ox. Three wolves chased many oxen. This person was watching a hippo. These people were watching some hippos.
This class of children likes that puppy best. Both classes of children like those puppies best.

TEACH

Show the first two sentences of the focus text. Look at the highlighted words. Ask: Are these singular or plural nouns? How do you know? [e.g. –s/–es endings; the determiners – 'three' and 'many' signal plural]. Repeat the question with the remaining paired sentences, discussing the highlighted nouns and the determiners used with them.

Revise the terms 'singular' [one] and 'plural' [more than one]. Explain that most nouns have a singular form and a plural form. Usually plural nouns are formed by adding –s or –es to the singular form [hippo/hippos, class/classes]. Sometimes this involves a change of spelling [e.g. wolf/wolves; puppy/puppies].

Remind the pupils that some plurals do not follow the normal –s/–es pattern [ox/oxen, person/people, child/children]. Explain that these are called irregular plurals. Discuss some more irregular plurals [e.g. mice; geese], or nouns that are the same in singular and plural [e.g. fish; sheep].

Explain that some determiners also have singular and plural forms [e.g. this/these]. Determiners can also indicate plurals by showing number [e.g. three] or quantity [e.g. some; many; both].

Use the phrase 'a class of children' to introduce the term 'collective noun'. Explain that a collective noun refers to a whole group of things and is used with a singular determiner [e.g. a class/one class/this class].

Invite the pupils to rework some of the focus text using collective nouns [e.g. a pack of wolves; a crowd of people; a litter of puppies].

EXTEND Discuss nouns that do not have a plural [e.g. butter; milk; cotton; wool; money; sadness].

PRACTISE
Pupil book page 22

APPLY
- The pupils write sentences with lists of animals using plural forms [e.g. … are all reptiles/mammals].
- Challenge the pupils to research or invent collective nouns for groups of animals, people or objects.
- The pupils use adjectives and plural nouns to write an 'A–Z' of Amazing Animals [e.g. fantastic flamingos], Incredible Nature [e.g. vicious volcanoes] or Fabulous Food [e.g. lovely loaves of bread].
- In science, the pupils list components using plural forms [e.g. bulbs; batteries].
- When writing reports, encourage the conscious use of singular and plural forms [e.g. a; some; many].
- Remind the pupils to use a dictionary to check plural forms of nouns [e.g. nouns ending 'o'].

ASSESS
Dictation: The women grew potatoes, carrots and radishes. The tubs were full of strawberries and tomatoes as red as rubies.
Say: Underline the irregular plural noun.
Check: All plural nouns are spelt correctly.

Pupil book answers

Singular and plural nouns

Remember

Most **plural nouns** are formed by adding **–s** or **–es** to the **singular** noun. Sometimes a change of spelling is needed.

a hippo   some hippos
a wolf   three wolves

Some plurals do not end with –s or –es. They are irregular plurals.

an ox   many oxen

Try it

1 Write the correct **plural** for each **noun**.

one potato	two	_potatoes_	one loaf	two	_loaves_
one gentleman	three	_gentlemen_	one hero	three	_heroes_
a mouth	many	_mouths_	a tooth	many	_teeth_
a switch	both	_switches_	a battery	both	_batteries_
a deer	a herd of	_deer_	a fish	a shoal of	_fish_

2 Rewrite each sentence with **plural nouns** rather than **singular** nouns.

One person took a photo of the one flamingo.
Some people took photos of the many flamingos.

An atlas, a dictionary or an encyclopedia is called a reference book.
Atlases, dictionaries and encyclopedias are called reference books.

That elf over there helped this woman to catch the thief.
Those elves over there helped these women to catch the thieves.

Sentence practice

Write <u>three</u> sentences about a farm and its animals, using as many **plural nouns** as you can.

The farmer keeps cows, goats, calves and sheep in the fields. Children
often visit the stables to ride the horses and ponies. In the farmyard,
there are ducks and geese.

22

These words are in line with current spelling expectations.

The plurals should be spelt correctly. 'Deer' and 'fish' are examples of nouns that are the same in the singular and plural forms.

As well as the nouns, check that the determiners and verbs have been changed to plural forms [e.g. is/are; this/these].

The plurals should be spelt correctly. 'Flamingos'/ 'flamingoes' is an example of a noun where there are two acceptable spellings. This is also true of some other words ending with 'o'.

This is just an example of possible sentences including some irregular plurals [e.g. geese; children] as well as a number of regular ones. Check that commas are used correctly in sentences with lists or fronted adverbials.

Lesson 16 Plural –s or possessive –'s?

Focus clarifying the difference between plural –s and possessive –'s; revising apostrophes for singular possession

Key terms apostrophe, **possession/possessive**, noun, singular, plural

Focus text The crews scientists scanned rows of screens showing data from stars and faraway galaxies. The ships computers could detect signals from distant planets.

TEACH

Show the focus text and read it aloud. Discuss details that show the setting is on board a spaceship, referring to the underlined noun phrases.

Ask the pupils if they notice anything missing from two of the underlined phrases. Give the clue that it is a punctuation mark [possessive apostrophe – in 'crews' and 'ships'].

Remind the pupils that we add an apostrophe with the letter 's' [–'s] to the end of a noun or proper noun to show possession – that something belongs to someone [e.g. Captain Kirk's spaceship is the spaceship belonging to Captain Kirk]. This makes a possessive noun.

Explain that people often confuse the possessive –'s with the –s added to form plurals. They add an apostrophe to the plural form of a noun just because it ends with –s. When adding –s to a noun, it is important to be clear about whether it is a plural –s [no apostrophe] or possessive –'s [with apostrophe].

Point to the noun 'crews' in the focus text. Ask: Does this show possession? Look at the next word [scientists]. Do the scientists belong to the crew? They do, so an apostrophe is needed. Write it in.

Do the same with a plural noun [e.g. rows]. Demonstrate that this word does not show possession; it simply means that there is more than one row. So it does *not* need an apostrophe. Ask the pupils where the other missing apostrophe should go [the ship's computers – the computers belong to the ship].

EXTEND Discuss how apostrophes are used with plural nouns that already end in –s [e.g. the scientists' computers]. [Note: This is the focus of the next lesson, Lesson 17.]

PRACTISE

Pupil book page 23

APPLY

• Encourage the pupils to look for plural –s and possessive –'s in the titles of stories [e.g. George's Marvellous Medicine; Mufaro's Beautiful Daughters; The Thief's Daughter; The Finders].
• Remind the pupils to check for overuse of apostrophes when proofreading. Encourage them to use the questions introduced above to check whether an apostrophe is needed.
• The pupils write ingredients for spells or potions using both plural and possessive nouns [e.g. six feathers; a bee's sting].
• Encourage the pupils to look for use – and misuse – of apostrophes in the environment [e.g. on signs, posters and labels].

ASSESS

Dictation: The boy's shoes and socks were left under the pegs. He saw the girls leave their coats and bags in Miss Black's classroom.
Check: The correct words and no others have apostrophes.

Pupil book answers

Plural –s or possessive –'s?

Remember

You add the letter **–s** to a **singular noun** to make a **plural** noun.

star**s**   planet**s**   moon**s**

You add an '**apostrophe s**' (**–'s**) to a singular noun to make it a **possessive** noun. This shows that something belongs to someone or something.

Captain Kirk**'s** spaceship   the ship**'s** computers

Try it

1 Add the letter **–s** or **–'s** ('**apostrophe s**') to each **noun**.

the straw man _'s_ trousers   the queen _'s_ three daughter _s_

two sack _s_ of gold   six tray _s_ of cake _s_

the writer _'s_ pen   the baby _'s_ toy _s_

the cat _'s_ basket   a zebra _'s_ stripe _s_

many pot _s_ of paint   the singer _'s_ new song _s_

my friend _'s_ band   the spider _'s_ eight leg _s_

If the pupils find it difficult to decide which words require 'apostrophe s', encourage them to try saying 'the ... belonging to the ...' [e.g. 'the toys belonging to the baby']. In some cases, the determiner before the noun gives a clue [e.g. many pots; two sacks].

2 Rewrite each sentence, using an **apostrophe** correctly.

Granddads hen's lay six eggs a day.   _Granddad's hens lay six eggs a day._

Bird's circled above the islands trees.   _Birds circled above the island's trees._

The old mans dog's ate all the pies.   _The old man's dogs ate all the pies._

The girls rode on the dragons back.   _The girls rode on the dragon's back._

Thieves stole the princes favourite golden slippers.
Thieves stole the prince's favourite golden slippers.

Tears ran down my little brothers cheek's when he fell over.
Tears ran down my little brother's cheeks when he fell over.

Each sentence needs one apostrophe for singular possession.

Check that the pupils have removed apostrophes from any plural words.

Sentence practice

Write a sentence about an elephant. Use a **plural** and a **possessive –'s**.

The little elephant's ears were large and floppy.

23

This is just an example of a possible sentence. Check that the apostrophe has been used correctly to show possession and that there is no apostrophe in the plural word.

Lesson 17 Apostrophes for plural possession 1

Focus apostrophe for plural possession [with regular plurals]

Key terms noun, apostrophe, possessive noun, singular, plural

Focus text Mr Moore's classroom   head teacher's office
             teachers' staffroom   parents' noticeboard

TEACH

Show the first two school 'signs' in the focus text. Ask the pupils to explain why an apostrophe is used in these signs [to show possession – e.g. it is the classroom belonging to Mr Moore]. Discuss why we use possessives like these. For example, ask: Why have a sign saying 'head teacher's office' rather than 'the office of the head teacher'? [e.g. it is shorter; easier to say]

Show the remaining signs. Explain that these signs also use apostrophes to show possession. Ask the pupils if they can see anything different [the placement of the apostrophe]. Discuss each sign, exploring how this time the item belongs to more than one person [e.g. the staffroom belongs to all the teachers, rather than just one; the noticeboard belongs to all the parents].

Remind the pupils that we add an apostrophe and the letter 's' to the end of a singular noun or proper noun to form a possessive noun [e.g. Mr Moore's classroom; the head teacher's office].

Explain that when there is more than one owner, the plural noun may already end in –s, so we just add the apostrophe, this time *after* the –s, to form the possessive noun. For example, with 'teachers' staffroom', we add the apostrophe after the whole word 'teachers', to show that the room belongs to many teachers.

Invite the pupils to suggest further school or classroom signs illustrating singular and plural possession [e.g. boys'/girls' toilets; the teacher's desk; the pupils' folders].

EXTEND Explain that with irregular plurals not ending in –s, we still add 'apostrophe s' [–'s] rather than just –s [e.g. the children's lunchboxes]. [Note: This is the focus of the next lesson, Lesson 18.]

PRACTISE

Pupil book page 24

APPLY

- The pupils write descriptions using singular and plural possessive nouns [e.g. the trees' branches were …; all the house's windows were …].
- The pupils use singular and plural possessive nouns when writing factual texts in other curriculum areas [e.g. Cats' teeth are …; A shark's teeth are …].
- The pupils write a biography using possessive apostrophes [e.g. David's father; his cousin's house].
- The pupils write signs for the classroom using possessive apostrophes with singular and plural nouns [e.g. Red Group's maths books].
- The pupils invent an animal made up of parts belonging to other animals [e.g. a cat's paws; parrots' feathers].

ASSESS

Dictation: The bear dipped her paw into the bees' honey. The bear's paw was sticky with sweet honey.
Check: The apostrophes are correctly placed.

Pupil book answers

Apostrophes for plural possession 1

Remember

To show **possession**, you add 'apostrophe s' (–'s) to a **singular noun**.

Mr Moore's classroom   head teacher's office

But if there is more than one owner and the **plural noun** already ends in 's', you just add an **apostrophe**.

teachers' staffroom   parents' noticeboard

Try it

1. Add a **possessive apostrophe** to each sentence. Add –'s to the end of **singular** nouns, and just an apostrophe to the end of **plural** nouns.

   I listened to my clock <u>'s</u> slow tick.

   The witches <u>'</u> conversation was interrupted.

   I must clean out the hamsters <u>'</u> cage.

   He was the emperor <u>'s</u> favourite son.

   Mum was late for the parents <u>'</u> meeting at school.

   The drivers <u>'</u> cars were all lined up on the starting grid.

   > Check that the pupils have added –'s and not –s' to the singular nouns.

2. Rewrite each phrase, using an **apostrophe** to show **plural possession**.

the bikes belonging to the boys	the boys' bikes
the father of the twins	the twins' father
the surgery belonging to the doctors	the doctors' surgery
the car belonging to her parents	her parents' car
the chairs belonging to the pupils	the pupils' chairs
the tractors belonging to the farmers	the farmers' tractors

   > If necessary, the pupils could orally rehearse the phrases before writing them. Check the apostrophe is placed after the letter 's'. You could discuss how this leaves the plural noun unaltered [e.g. the boys'].

Sentence practice

Write a sentence about something belonging to some girls. Use an **apostrophe**.

The girls' paintings were hanging on the wall.

24

This is just an example of a sentence using an apostrophe to show plural possession.

Lesson 18 Apostrophes for plural possession 2

Focus apostrophe for plural possession [with irregular plurals]

Key terms apostrophe, plural noun, singular noun

Focus text the boys' egg and spoon race   the children's mini-marathon
the girls' obstacle race   the men's 10km run
the ladies' sprint   the women's 10km run

TEACH

Show the first list of events in the focus text. Ask the pupils to explain why an apostrophe is used in these phrases [to show possession – the race/sprint is for boys/girls/ladies]. Discuss why just an apostrophe is added rather than –'s [because 'boys', 'girls', 'ladies' are plural nouns and they already end with –s].

Show the second list of events. Discuss why the apostrophes are used here [again, to show plural possession – the mini-marathon is for children]. Ask the pupils if they notice anything different [e.g. 'apostrophe s' has been added to these plural nouns; these plurals do not end with –s; they are irregular plurals].

Remind the pupils that when a plural noun ends with –s, we just add an apostrophe to show possession. Explain that if a plural noun does *not* end in –s, then we add 'apostrophe s' [–'s] to show possession, just as we do after a singular noun.

Some pupils may find these rules confusing. Use the focus text to show how to check that the apostrophe is in the right place. Tell the pupils to look at what is written *before* the apostrophe. It should be the *full* name of the possessor[s] [e.g. 'men' in 'the men's 10km'; 'ladies' in 'the ladies' sprint']. Write some more phrases to demonstrate that this works with both plural and singular possession [e.g. a winner's medal].

Invite the pupils to suggest events for an animal Olympics, using possessive noun phrases with regular and irregular plurals [e.g. the kangaroos' high jump; the mice's obstacle race].

EXTEND Write rules to summarise the correct use of the possessive apostrophe.

PRACTISE

Pupil book page 25

APPLY

- The pupils write a news story about a department store, mentioning different departments [e.g. ladies' sportswear; men's clothing; children's toys].
- The pupils make posters listing events and competitions, using possessive apostrophes [e.g. a children's treasure hunt; a parents' dancing competition].
- Focus on the use of apostrophes when the pupils are writing historical reports [e.g. The peasants' houses ...].
- When the pupils are proofreading, remind them to check the use of any possessive apostrophes, first by checking they show possession and then by looking at the noun before the apostrophe.

ASSESS

Dictation: Mice's tails are longer than their bodies but rats' tails are shorter. A rat's body is fatter than a mouse's body.
Check: The four apostrophes are correctly placed.

Pupil book answers

Apostrophes for plural possession 2

Remember

To show **plural possession**, if the plural noun already ends in 's', you just add an **apostrophe**.

the boys' egg and spoon race   the girls' obstacle race

But if the **plural noun** does not end in 's', you add '**apostrophe s**' (–'s).

the men's 10km run   the women's 10km run

Try it

1 The underlined nouns are plurals but they do not end in 's'. Rewrite each phrase, using an **apostrophe** to show possession.

the helmets belonging to the <u>policemen</u>   the policemen's helmets

the art competition for <u>children</u>   the children's art competition

the decision of the <u>people</u>   the people's decision

the tails belonging to the <u>mice</u>   the mice's tails

2 All the nouns in these sentences are plural. Rewrite each sentence adding **apostrophes** in the correct place.

The shepherds shears set to work on the sheeps thick coats.

The shepherds' shears set to work on the sheep's thick coats.

I was more scared of the geeses sharp beaks than the guard dogs vicious teeth.

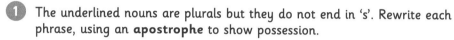
I was more scared of the geese's sharp beaks than the guard dogs'
vicious teeth.

The fishermens nets were full of fish but the childrens stomachs were still empty.

The fishermen's nets were full of fish but the children's stomachs were
still empty.

Sentence practice

Write a sentence about something belonging to some firemen. Use an **apostrophe**.

The firemen's hose was long enough to reach the burning building.

25

There should be two apostrophes added in each sentence to show plural possession. Check that other plural nouns are not given apostrophes [e.g. shears; beaks; stomachs].

Remind the pupils to look at what is written *before* the apostrophe to check that the possessive apostrophe is in the right place [e.g. 'guard <u>dogs</u>' vicious teeth' because there is more than one dog].

There will be further opportunities to reinforce the correct use of apostrophes later in the programme.

This is an example of a suitable sentence using an apostrophe to show plural possession.

Lesson 19 Standard English

Focus recognising spoken non-Standard verb forms and the equivalent Standard English forms

Key terms **Standard English, non-Standard verb form**, past tense

Focus text

1.
I hates begging but we be hungry, Sir. We was hopin' for a crust of bread.

2.
Yesterday, the baker gived us a bread roll. We broked it in half.

3.
It ain't much, one bread roll, when you're sweepin' the streets.

TEACH

Show the focus text. Read the speech bubbles aloud using suitable expression/voices for Victorian street children. Ask the pupils to picture the scene. Discuss the mental picture created.

Ask the pupils what makes it sound like informal speech. Underline phrases such as 'I hates begging' and 'we be hungry'. Ask the pupils if they recognise that these verb forms are not what we would normally expect to read.

Introduce the terms 'Standard English' and 'non-Standard English'. Explain that Standard English is the form of English generally used when writing. It is the English we find in books that we read and the English we should use in our writing. Non-Standard English is sometimes used in everyday speech.

The focus text shows some of the non-Standard verb forms that might be used in speech. Ask the pupils to identify the non-Standard verb forms used in each speech bubble and discuss the Standard English verb form in each case. Explain that although these non-Standard forms are sometimes used in speech, they should not be used in writing, unless there is a specific reason [e.g. writing a convincing dialogue].

Use speech bubble 1 to discuss the need for subject–verb agreement in Standard English [I hate, we are, we were]. Use speech bubble 2 to discuss the past tense form of irregular verbs needed in Standard English [gave, broke]. Use speech bubble 3 to discuss other non-Standard forms sometimes used in speech [ain't/isn't, sweepin'/sweeping].

The use of non-Standard verb forms varies depending on region and dialect. Focus your teaching on any non-Standard forms of verbs that your pupils use in their writing.

EXTEND Discuss the non-Standard forms that occur in your pupils' writing [e.g. them/those].

PRACTISE

Pupil book page 26

APPLY

- Encourage oral rehearsal of sentences before the pupils write them down using Standard English. Ask: How would we write that in a book? Does that sound like a book?
- Remind the pupils to use Standard English verb forms in all writing in other areas of the curriculum.
- The pupils write a short dialogue for a story, deliberately using non-Standard verb forms in the direct speech. They then rewrite it using Standard English.

ASSESS

Dictation: Dad teached me how to fly a kite. It were such fun. Now we goes to the park every Saturday.
Say: Rewrite the text using Standard English verb forms.
Answer: Dad taught me how to fly a kite. It was such fun. Now we go to the park every Saturday.

Pupil book answers

Standard English

Remember

Non-Standard English is sometimes used in speech but in writing you should nearly always use **Standard English verb forms**.

We <u>was hopin'</u> for some bread.   We were hoping for some bread.
The baker <u>gived</u> us a bread roll.   The baker gave us a bread roll.

Try it

1 Rewrite each sentence using **Standard English verb forms**.

I hates waiting around.	I hate waiting around.
He speaked to me yesterday.	He spoke to me yesterday.
They ain't comin' to my party.	They aren't coming to my party.
She catched a cold last week.	She caught a cold last week.
I weren't hungry.	I wasn't hungry.

Check that the contraction in the third sentence is spelt correctly with the apostrophe in the correct place.

2 Underline the **non-Standard verb forms** used in the text below.

It <u>ain't</u> fair. Our team should <u>of</u> won. We <u>was</u> unlucky. We <u>gived</u> a goal away right at the end. I <u>hates</u> losing like that. It <u>make</u> me very angry.

Now rewrite the text using **Standard English verb forms**.

It isn't fair. Our team should have won. We were unlucky. We gave a goal away right at the end. I hate losing like that. It makes me very angry.

Use this activity to remind the pupils to check the verbs in their own writing, by recognising what does not sound right and then correcting it. Focus attention on any non-Standard verb forms that your pupils use in their writing.

Sentence practice

Write <u>two</u> sentences about waiting for breaktime, using **non-Standard verb forms**. Then rewrite them using **Standard English verb forms**.

We was waitin' for the bell to ring but it taked forever. Then we runned outside and throwed a tennis ball to each other.

We were waiting for the bell to ring but it took forever. Then we ran outside and threw a tennis ball to each other.

Read the two versions aloud to compare the different effects.

26

These are just examples of sentences showing the use of non-Standard and Standard verb forms.

Apostrophes should be used correctly in any contractions.

Lesson 20 Verbs: perfect form

> **Focus** the Standard form of irregular verbs in the perfect tense
>
> **Key terms** Standard English, verb, past tense, perfect form
>
> **Focus text** **Vicky:** I have been very busy. I have throwed all my dirty clothes in the wash. I have writ my spellings out. I have began my maths.
>
> **Johnny:** I done all my homework and I been shopping with Mum. I seen my friend at the supermarket.

TEACH

Show the focus text and read it aloud. Ask: Are the characters talking about things they have done in the past, things they are doing right now or things they will do in the future? [things done in the past]

Read aloud Vicky's speech. Ask the pupils if this sounds like Standard English. Why not? [the verbs 'throwed', 'writ', 'began'] Ask for and write in the Standard English verb forms [thrown, written, begun].

Read aloud Johnny's speech. Ask: Is this in Standard English? [no, it should be 'I have done' or 'I did'] Add the verb 'have' before the verbs in both sentences [have done, have been, have seen] and reread Johnny's speech.

Explain that the focus text uses the perfect form of verbs, which we use to refer to events that have happened in the past and/or are still important now.

Remind the pupils that the perfect form of verbs uses the verb 'have' [with 'I'/'you'/'we'/'they'] or 'has' [with 'he'/'she'/'it'], together with the main verb [e.g. walked; done]. Explain that sometimes the main verb is the same in the perfect tense as it is in the simple past tense [e.g. have walked/walked], but many common verbs have a special spelling that we only use with 'have'/'has' in perfect forms [e.g. 'have thrown', not 'have threw'; 'have written' – not 'have wrote'; 'have begun', not 'have began'].

Explain that it is important to know the Standard English verb forms to use with the verb 'have'/'has'. It is also important not to confuse them with simple past tense verbs and use them *without* 'have'/'has', as Johnny does in the focus text [e.g. I done all my homework.].

EXTEND Discuss other verbs that have different simple past tense and perfect forms [e.g. chose/chosen].

PRACTISE

Pupil book page 27

APPLY

- Encourage the use of the perfect form of verbs in accounts, letters, diary events and to talk about past events [e.g. I have been ...; I have done ...; I have been looking forward to ...].
- The pupils use perfect forms in an information text, report or magazine article, to show how past events relate to now [e.g. If you have eaten ...].
- The pupils use the perfect form of verbs when writing the thoughts and feelings of a character reflecting on events that have happened [e.g. I have hidden the treasure. I have not forgotten.].
- Identify perfect verb forms when reading with the pupils, drawing attention to the correct spelling.

ASSESS

Dictation: Snow fell overnight. Both the ponds froze.
Say: Rewrite these sentences using the perfect form of the verbs.
Answer: Snow has fallen overnight. Both the ponds have frozen.

Pupil book answers

Verbs: perfect form

Remember

The **perfect form** of **verbs** is used to write about things that have happened in the recent past and/or are still important now. The perfect form uses the verb '**has**' or '**have**' and a main verb in the **past tense**. Sometimes, a special form of the main verb is used.

I have been very busy.
I have done all my homework.

Try it

1 Choose the correct **perfect verb form** for each sentence.

I have _____ eaten _____ six chocolate biscuits.   (ate eat eaten)

I have _____ seen _____ this film before.   (saw seen see)

Sorry, I have _____ forgotten _____ your name.   (forget forgot forgotten)

Someone has _____ broken _____ Mum's antique vase.   (broken break broke)

We have _____ drawn _____ this picture for you.   (draw drawn drew)

The teacher has _____ rung _____ the bell.   (ringed rang rung)

Someone has _____ stolen _____ all my money.   (stolen steal stole)

> This activity helps to introduce the pupils to the correct perfect form of some common verbs.

2 Rewrite each sentence using the **perfect form** of the underlined **verbs**.

I have drank my juice and Dad have drank his coffee.
 I have drunk my juice and Dad has drunk his coffee.

I have spoke to the manager and we have writ a letter.
 I have spoken to the manager and we have written a letter.

All the leaves have fell off the trees and the birds has flew away.
 All the leaves have fallen off the trees and the birds have flown away.

> If the pupils are not familiar with the correct verb forms, encourage them to orally rehearse the sentences before writing them.
>
> Make lists of irregular verbs that have different simple past tense and perfect forms for the pupils to refer to [e.g. drank/drunk; spoke/spoken].

Sentence practice

Write a sentence about something that grew in a garden. Use a **perfect verb form**.

 Lots of weeds have grown in the garden.

27

This is just an example of a sentence using the perfect form of 'grow'.

Revision 2 answers

This page revises terms and word classes introduced in **Grammar 3** and Section 1 of this book.

The focus of each activity is given to help you identify areas where the pupils might need further revision.

Focus: determiners, including the correct use of 'a' and 'an'

Other answers are possible [e.g. ... my sack is lighter than your sack]. An appropriate determiner must be used with singular/plural nouns.

Check that the determiners at the start of sentences start with capital letters. Check the use of 'a' and 'an'.

Focus: appropriate use of pronouns

Focus: expressing time and place using prepositions; knowledge of the term 'adverbial'

These are just examples. Compare the pupils' answers to find the most interesting or effective sentence.

Check that a comma is added after the fronted adverbials.

Revision 2

1 Complete the sentences below using a different **determiner** in each space.

_____A_____ mouse is much smaller than _____an_____ elephant.

_____Some_____ dogs are working animals but _____many_____ dogs are kept as pets.

_____The_____ man said, "I think _____this_____ sack is lighter than _____that_____ sack."

We have _____some_____ apple trees in _____our_____ front garden.

Yesterday _____my_____ brother gave us _____his_____ old skateboard.

2 Rewrite each sentence using **pronouns** in place of the underlined nouns and noun phrases.

The children had a card for Dad.   They had a card for him.

Adam and I found the flower pots outside.   We found them outside.

The lorry nearly hit the old lady.   It nearly hit her.

Emily was quicker than Max and me.   She was quicker than us.

Mohsin waited for his grandparents.   He waited for them.

3 Complete each sentence by adding an **adverbial** that starts with a **preposition**.

The man disappeared through the window.

The fire began between six and seven o'clock.

A helicopter hovered above the treetops.

_____On the doorstep,_____ there was a big box.

_____On the table,_____ there was a plate of fish and chips.

4 Underline the **conjunction** in each sentence.

They clung to the rope while the eagle circled overhead.

As Jack sat on the riverbank, he heard someone cough.

The lightning flashed immediately after we heard the thunder.

Although she was tired, Shivani finished her book before bedtime.

Focus: recognising conjunctions

In the fourth sentence, check that only the word 'although' is underlined. The word 'before' is used as a preposition in this sentence – it is followed by a noun [bedtime].

The pupils may well still find conjunctions and prepositions confusing, but these topics will be covered again in **Grammar 5**.

This page revises work on verb forms covered in earlier books and terms relating to sentences introduced in **Grammar 3** and reinforced in this book.

The focus of each activity is given to help you identify areas where the pupils might need further revision.

5 Rewrite each sentence using the **past progressive form** of the underlined **verb**.

The cat <u>hid</u> in the bushes.   The cat was hiding in the bushes.

I <u>sat</u> next to Sophie.   I was sitting next to Sophie.

They <u>swept</u> the leaves.   They were sweeping the leaves.

We <u>went</u> to school.   We were going to school.

She <u>ate</u> her noodles.   She was eating her noodles.

6 There is an error in each sentence. Rewrite the sentences correctly.

Yesterday, Mrs Patel took her cakes to the market and she sells them all.

Yesterday, Mrs Patel took her cakes to the market and she sold them all.

Last week, I went to the cinema with my best friend and we see a film.

Last week, I went to the cinema with my best friend and we saw a film.

7 Underline the **main clause** in each sentence.

<u>The dog began to bark</u> before I even opened the gate.

Unfortunately, <u>the plants did not grow</u> as it was too cold.

As the train approached the station, <u>Mia was very excited</u>.

<u>I was scared</u> when I heard the noise.

<u>Uncle Andrew arrived</u> while I was asleep.

8 Rewrite each sentence, adding a **subordinate clause**.

The car skidded.

The car skidded when the driver braked.

The beast slept soundly.

While the music was playing, the beast slept soundly.

Austin played outside.

Austin played outside until it was time for bed.

Focus: subordinating conjunctions and subordinate clauses

These are just examples of grammatically correct sentences containing subordinate clauses. The sentences must use correct punctuation, including a comma if the subordinate clause is put at the start of the sentence.

Compare the pupils' answers.

Focus: use of the past progressive form of verbs

This was introduced in **Grammar 2** but the term 'progressive form' was only introduced in **Grammar 3**. Remind the pupils that this refers to the –ing form of the verb. In the past tense, it is used with 'was'/'were'.

Terms related to verb forms will continue to be reinforced.

Focus: correct choice and consistent use of past tense

The adverbs [e.g. Yesterday] indicate that the past tense is the appropriate choice. Use this activity to remind the pupils to check for tense consistency when editing their work.

Focus: identifying main clauses

Remind the pupils that the main clause is the part that makes sense on its own and could be a complete sentence. This activity shows that main clauses can be found in different positions.

29

Writing task 2: Analysis sheet

Tick the circles to show amount of evidence found in writing:
1 No evidence
2 Some evidence
3 Clear evidence ✓

Pupil name: _____

Date: _____

Assessing punctuation

The writing sample demonstrates:	Evidence		
sentence boundaries demarcated with capital letters and appropriate end punctuation.	1	2	3
capital letters used for 'I' and proper nouns [e.g. Roman times; King Arthur].	1	2	3
commas used to separate items in a list.	1	2	3
apostrophes used in contracted forms or for singular and plural possession [e.g. the children's clothes].	1	2	3
inverted commas and other punctuation marks used in direct speech [e.g. "Who are you?" he asked.].	1	2	3
commas used after fronted adverbials – adverbs, phrases or clauses [e.g. When I looked round, …].	1	2	3

Assessing grammar and sentence structure

The writing sample demonstrates:	Evidence		
grammatically correct sentences [e.g. noun–verb agreement; Standard English verb forms].	1	2	3
a variety of sentence types [e.g. exclamations and questions – 'What a sight!'; 'Where was I?'].	1	2	3
sentences with more than one clause; a range of subordinating conjunctions to expand ideas.	1	2	3
correct and consistent use of the past tense when recounting the events.	1	2	3
the accurate use of pronouns to avoid repetition and to make links.	1	2	3
adverbials to add detail about events – where, when, how [e.g. slowly; in the corner], and to vary sentence openings.	1	2	3
expanded noun phrases to describe and add detail about people and settings.	1	2	3

Key target: _____

Writing task 2: Pupil checklist

Name: _____   Date: _____

Reread what you have written to check that it makes sense. Tick the circle if you have correctly used the punctuation or grammar feature in your writing.

Punctuation

◯ I have used capital letters and full stops to punctuate sentences.

◯ I have used question marks or exclamation marks where needed.

◯ I have used capital letters for 'I' and any names.

◯ I have used commas to separate items in a list.

◯ I have used apostrophes only in contracted forms (e.g. they weren't) and for possession (e.g. the children's clothes).

◯ I have used correct punctuation for direct speech (e.g. "Who are you?" I asked.).

◯ I have used commas after fronted adverbials (e.g. When I looked round, ...).

Grammar and sentences

◯ I have written in sentences and used Standard English verb forms.

◯ I have used different sentence types (e.g. questions, exclamations).

◯ I have used sentences with more than one clause and a range of conjunctions to develop ideas.

◯ I have used the past tense to write about what happened.

◯ I have used pronouns to avoid repetition and their meaning is clear.

◯ I have used adverbials to add detail about events – where, when or how.

◯ I have used different sentence starters (e.g. adverbs, prepositional phrases).

◯ I have used longer noun phrases to describe and give details.

Teacher feedback

My key target: _____

_____

Lesson 21 Possessive pronouns

Focus introducing possessive pronouns

Key terms possession/possessive, determiner, noun, noun phrase, pronoun, **possessive pronoun**

Focus text
This is my book.	This is mine.
This is your book.	This is yours.
That is her painting.	That is hers.
That is his painting.	That is his.
Those are our folders.	Those are ours.
Those are their folders.	Those are theirs.

TEACH

Show the sentences in the first column of the focus text. Read each sentence aloud, emphasising the highlighted words and pointing to appropriate objects and people in the room [e.g. yourself for 'my'; a pupil for 'your']. Discuss what type of word is highlighted [e.g. determiners – they are used before nouns; possessives – they show possession or ownership].

Show the second column of the focus text. Again, read each sentence aloud emphasising the highlighted words and pointing to appropriate people to clarify their meaning. Explain that these are possessives too but they are also pronouns, because they stand in place of noun phrases [e.g. This is my book. This is mine.].

Explain that all of the highlighted words are used when talking about possession or ownership – who things belong to. Explain that in the first column some of the highlighted words [e.g. her; his; our] replace possessive nouns, or names with a possessive apostrophe [e.g. Becky's painting/her painting; Danny's painting/his painting; my group's folders/our folders]. As these words are followed by a noun, they are being used as determiners in noun phrases. Underline these noun phrases [e.g. my book; your book].

In the second column, the highlighted words again show possession but these words stand alone – they have no noun after them. Instead, they replace a noun phrase, so they are pronouns [e.g. This is your book. This is yours.]. Explain that 'mine', 'yours', 'hers', 'his', 'ours', and 'theirs' are possessive pronouns.

EXTEND Discuss the possessive pronoun 'its'. This is more often used as a determiner with a noun [e.g. the book's cover/its cover]. Discuss the difference between possessive 'its' [belonging to 'it'] and contracted 'it's' [it is].

PRACTISE

Pupil book page 32

APPLY

- The pupils write personal letters [e.g. to a real or imaginary pen friend] using possessive pronouns to ask and answer questions [e.g. My teacher is called Mr Marshall. What about yours?].
- The pupils act out and then write a scene where a group of children sort out a box of long-lost possessions, using as many possessive pronouns as they can [e.g. Look! This old teddy is yours.].
- The pupils write list poems using possessive pronouns [e.g. This world is ours/yours; The deepest oceans are ours/yours].

ASSESS

Dictation: We put all our lunchboxes on the bench. I knew mine was the red one.
Say: Underline the possessive pronoun.

58

Pupil book answers

Possessive pronouns

Remember

Pronouns stand in place of **nouns** or **noun phrases**. Possessive pronouns are the words 'mine', 'yours', 'his', 'hers', 'ours', 'theirs' and 'its'.

That is <u>Becky's painting</u>. That painting is hers.
That is <u>Danny's painting</u>. That painting is his.

Try it

1 Add the missing **possessive pronoun** to complete each sentence.

Those PE bags belong to us. They are ___ours___ .

That ruler belongs to you. It is ___yours___ .

That tent belongs to Lauren. It is ___hers___ .

Those trainers belong to me. They are ___mine___ .

That jumper belongs to Liam. It is ___his___ .

That atlas belongs to Class 4. It is ___theirs___ .

2 Write a **possessive pronoun** to replace the underlined noun phrase.

I've found your coat. Have you seen <u>my coat</u>?	mine
Jordan lost his swimming trunks. These must be <u>Jordan's trunks</u>.	his
My sister is called Maryam and this is <u>her bike</u>.	hers
My favourite team is Leicester City. What's <u>your favourite team</u>?	yours
We love your poster. Do you like <u>our poster</u>?	ours
Our models are bigger than <u>that group's models</u>.	theirs

Sentence practice

Write <u>three</u> sentences about who owns which book. Use **possessive pronouns**.

The book about tigers is mine. The book about Ancient Egypt is yours.

This dictionary is his and that one is hers.

32

This activity helps to introduce the pupils to the possessive pronouns 'mine', 'yours', 'his', 'hers', 'ours', 'theirs'.

Check that there is no apostrophe in these words [e.g. our's]. This is a common error as pupils are used to using 'apostrophe s' to show possession.

If necessary, the pupils could orally rehearse the sentences with the possessive pronouns.

These are just examples of sentences using possessive pronouns. Check that the pupils use possessive pronouns [mine, yours, hers, his, ours, theirs] and not a possessive determiner and noun [e.g. my book about tigers; her dictionary]. If they do make this mistake, help them to reword the sentence using the appropriate possessive pronouns [mine, hers].

Lesson 22 Making pronouns clear

> Focus recognising when the meaning of a pronoun is unclear; making changes to clarify meaning
>
> Key terms pronoun, noun, noun phrase, proper noun, direct speech
>
> Focus text Scarlett was going for a walk with Ellie. She had her little sister with her. As they walked along the path, they saw a ten pound note. She said that it was hers.

TEACH

Show the focus text and read it aloud. Ask questions that focus on understanding who the pronouns refer to. For example, ask: Who was Scarlett going for a walk with? [Ellie] Who had her little sister with her, Scarlett or Ellie? [we don't know – it is unclear who 'she' is] Who walked along the path? [Scarlett, Ellie and the little sister] Who claimed the ten pound note? [we don't know – it is unclear who 'she' is]

Discuss what type of word is highlighted [pronouns – personal pronouns and the possessive pronoun 'hers']. Ask the pupils why pronouns are a problem in this text [because it is not always clear who they refer to].

Remind the pupils that pronouns stand in place of nouns or noun phrases. We use pronouns to avoid repeating nouns and proper nouns. However, we must be careful not to use a pronoun if it is confusing or unclear which person or noun it refers to. Identify and underline the pronouns that are not clear in the focus text [she, her, hers].

Discuss how to change the focus text to make the meaning clear. Show that the first pronoun in a sentence can be changed back to a noun or name [e.g. Ellie had her little sister with her.]. Sometimes, we can use an alternative noun or noun phrase [e.g. As the girls walked along the path, they ...].

Discuss different ways of making the meaning of the last sentence clear – for example, reverting to using a name [e.g. Scarlett said that it was hers.] or using direct speech [e.g. "That's mine," said Scarlett.].

Invite the pupils to orally compose sentences to continue the focus text, choosing appropriate nouns or pronouns.

EXTEND Compare the use of direct speech [e.g. "That's mine," said Ellie.] and indirect speech [e.g. She said that it was hers.].

PRACTISE

Pupil book page 33

APPLY

- When the pupils are writing stories or accounts, remind them to keep rereading a paragraph or group of sentences to check that it is clear who or what a pronoun stands for.
- The pupils write a story with all male or all female characters, making sure to check that it is clear who the pronouns 'he'/'him'/'his' and 'she'/'her'/'hers' refer to.
- Add checking pronouns to the pupils' list of editing tasks. They should work with a partner to recognise when pronouns are confusing and then decide how to make the meaning clear.

ASSESS

Dictation: Chris and Tom are looking for their coats. Have you seen them?
Say: Underline the pronoun that could be confusing. Why is it confusing?
Answer: 'Them' could mean either Chris and Tom, or their coats.

Pupil book answers

Making pronouns clear

Remember

Pronouns can be used in place of **nouns** or **noun phrases** to help avoid repetition. However, you should only use a pronoun if it is clear which person or noun it refers to.

<u>Scarlett</u> was going to the funfair with <u>Ellie</u>. She had her little sister with her.   (unclear)

<u>Scarlett</u> was going to the funfair with <u>Ellie</u>. <u>Ellie</u> had her little sister with her.   (clear)

Try it

1 The **pronouns** in these sentences are confusing. Explain why.

Clara saw her grandmother when she was crossing the road.
'She' could be Clara or her grandmother, so the sentence is not clear.

When Matthew went exploring with Ben, he got very muddy.
'He' could be Matthew or Ben, so the sentence is not clear.

Dad took the clock off the shelf so he could mend it.
'It' could be either the clock or the shelf, so the sentence is not clear.

2 Rewrite each sentence in a way that makes the meaning clear.

Grace dropped the television on the glass table and it broke.
Grace dropped the television on the glass table and the table broke.

Mark asked Charlie if he could help him with the play.
"Can I help you with the play?" Mark asked Charlie.

Greg saw Mr Davies as he left the classroom.
Greg saw Mr Davies as the teacher left the classroom.

Sentence practice

Write a sentence about Maria and Katya, using **pronouns** that make the meaning clear.

Maria hurt her arm so Katya carried her bag for her.

33

You could discuss with the pupils how to make the sentences clear [e.g. Clara saw her grandmother when the old lady was crossing the road. When Matthew went exploring with Ben, Matthew got very muddy.].

The pupils may find different ways of making the meaning clear [e.g. Mark asked Charlie if he could help Charlie with the play.]. Compare the pupils' answers and discuss different possibilities.

This is just an example of a possible sentence. Here the context of the sentence makes it clear that 'her' refers to Maria.

Lesson 23 Co-ordinating and subordinating conjunctions

Focus distinguishing subordinating and co-ordinating conjunctions

Key terms **subordinating conjunction**, **co-ordinating conjunction**, main clause, subordinate clause

Focus text Simon opened the door and stepped inside. I fumbled for the switch but the light did not come on. We inched our way forward as it was dark inside. I tried to stay calm although my heart was beating fast. Once my eyes became used to the darkness, I could make out some large, shadowy shapes.

TEACH

Show the focus text and read it aloud. Discuss what makes it effective and helps build tension.

Ask the pupils what type of word is highlighted [conjunctions – used to join two words, phrases or clauses together in one sentence]. Discuss why the conjunctions are used and how they improve the text [e.g. they link events or expand on ideas; they make it sound better than using only short sentences].

Tell the pupils that conjunctions can be subordinating conjunctions or co-ordinating conjunctions. Explain that the words 'and', 'but', 'or' are co-ordinating conjunctions. They join together two words, phrases or clauses that are equally important. For example, in the focus text, 'and' links two equally important actions, while 'but' links two main clauses, which both make sense independently [I fumbled for the switch but the light did not come on.].

Explain that the words 'as', 'although', 'once' are subordinating conjunctions. They join a subordinate clause to a main clause. Remind the pupils that a subordinate clause adds extra information about the main clause [e.g. when or why it happened]. It is a less important clause than the main clause. Ask the pupils to identify examples of main and subordinate clauses in the focus text.

Use the last sentence of the focus text to remind the pupils that clauses starting with subordinating conjunctions can function as adverbials, so they can be fronted, or used at the start of a sentence.

EXTEND Discuss other of subordinating conjunctions used to show time [e.g. after; since; whilst] or to compare or contrast ideas [e.g. even though; unless; whereas].

PRACTISE

Pupil book page 34

APPLY

• Challenge the pupils to write six sentences on a given subject, using two co-ordinating conjunctions, two subordinating conjunctions and two sentences with no conjunctions.

• When the pupils are writing stories, encourage them to vary sentences by using both co-ordinating and subordinating conjunctions, as well as some short sentences for effect.

• The pupils convert notes into complete sentences using co-ordinating and subordinating conjunctions to link pieces of information [e.g. writing a comparison of two animals].

ASSESS

Dictation: Maya insisted on clearing the table <u>and</u> washing the plates after they finished eating.
Say: Underline the co-ordinating conjunction in this sentence.

Pupil book answers

Co-ordinating and subordinating conjunctions

Remember

The words 'and', 'but' and 'or' are **co-ordinating conjunctions**. They can join two words, phrases or **main clauses** of equal importance.

I fumbled for the switch but the light did not come on.

Subordinating conjunctions join a **subordinate** (less important) **clause** to a main clause, to add extra information about the main clause.

I tried to stay calm although my heart was beating fast.

Try it

1. Underline the **conjunction** in each sentence. Write '**C**' if it is a **co-ordinating** conjunction, or '**S**' if it is a **subordinating** conjunction.

   Yanwen went into the shop <u>and</u> she bought a new skateboard.   C

   I can't drink lemonade <u>as</u> the bubbles make me sneeze.   S

   <u>Once</u> you hear the whistle, run to the other side.   S

   Give me a hand <u>or</u> the kite will get tangled in the tree.   C

2. Use a **co-ordinating conjunction** to add another **main clause**.

   Nina was exhausted _but she kept going to the top of the hill._

   Jason picked some apples _and he took them into the kitchen._

   Now use a **subordinating conjunction** to add a **subordinate clause**.

   Nina was exhausted _after she climbed the hill._

   Jason picked some apples _because he wanted to make a pie._

Sentence practice

Write <u>two</u> sentences about a snake. Use a **co-ordinating conjunction** in the first sentence and a **subordinating conjunction** in the second.

The python slowly uncoiled and slithered along a branch. The boy

heard the python hiss although he could not see it.

34

Check that the pupils recognise the subordinating conjunction 'once' used at the start of the third sentence.

These are just examples of sentences using co-ordinating conjunctions.

Similarly, the second set are examples of sentences using subordinating conjunctions. The pupils should now know a range of subordinating conjunctions, so encourage them to use a different conjunction in each sentence.

This is just an example of two sentences using a co-ordinating conjunction and then a subordinating conjunction.

Lesson 24 Giving reasons: cause and effect

Focus   extending the range of words used to express cause and effect

Key terms   conjunction, preposition, noun phrase, adverb

Focus text   **The main road is closed due to an accident.**
Clark Street is also closed so that the police can get to the scene.
The roads will be closed for some time and therefore a diversion has been put in place.

TEACH

Show the focus text. Read each sentence and discuss the reason for that event [e.g. Why is the main road closed? Why is Clark Street closed? Why is a diversion needed?]. Underline the part of each sentence that tells us the reason [due to an accident, so that the police can get to the scene, The roads will be closed for some time].

Explain that when we want to give the reason for something we often use the conjunctions 'because', 'since' and 'as' to show the cause. Point out that the traffic news in the focus text could be given using these conjunctions [e.g. The main road is closed <u>because</u> there has been an accident. A diversion has been put in place <u>as</u> the roads will be closed for some time.].

Explain that the focus text shows some other words that can be used to give reasons or to show cause and effect. The first sentence shows a preposition that we can use to introduce a cause [due to]. As it is a preposition, it is followed by a noun phrase [an accident]. Another preposition, 'because of', could be used in the same way [... <u>because of</u> an accident].

The second sentence shows another conjunction used to give a reason why: 'so that' shows the purpose or reason for an action [... <u>so that</u> police can get to the scene].

The third sentence demonstrates the use of the adverb 'therefore'. The sentence makes sense without this word but using it helps to show the cause and effect more clearly [the roads are closed and <u>for that reason</u> there is a diversion]. The cause comes first and the effect second, as with the conjunction 'so'. Usually, 'therefore' links two separate sentences. Here it is used with 'and' to link the ideas in one sentence.

EXTEND   Discuss which sentences could be reordered to place the reason at the start or front of the sentence [e.g. Due to an accident, the main road is closed.].

PRACTISE

Pupil book page 35

APPLY

- The pupils write news bulletins using prepositions, conjunctions and adverbs to explain reasons for events [e.g. The shop was closed because of the fire.].
- The pupils write letters setting out views and opinions on a current issue, discussing cause and effect.
- When the pupils are writing explanations in other subject areas, encourage them to use a range of words to give reasons and show cause and effect [e.g. The ice melted due to the higher temperature.].
- The pupils write poems or imaginative sentences beginning with the preposition 'because of'.

ASSESS

Dictation: The playgroup must close <u>because of</u> spending cuts. It will close at the end of the month as it is too expensive to run.

Say: Underline the preposition used to show cause.

Pupil book answers

Giving reasons: cause and effect

Remember

You can show the cause (the reason why something happens) by using **conjunctions** such as 'so that', **prepositions** such as 'due to' and **adverbs** such as 'therefore'.

The main road is closed due to an accident.
The road will be closed for some time and therefore a diversion has been put in place.

Try it

1 Choose a different word or phrase from the box to complete each sentence with a reason why.

> **because of**   **so that**   **for**   **as**   **therefore**

The crops did not grow _____because of_____ the drought.

He went to the leisure centre _____for_____ a swim.

The striker is injured and _____therefore_____ is unlikely to play.

Do not go near the cliff top _____as_____ it is dangerous.

She stood on a box _____so that_____ she could see over the wall.

2 Complete each sentence by adding a reason why.

The match was cancelled due to _player illness._

I could not concentrate because of _all the noise._

The werewolf stood in the doorway to _stop them from leaving._

Ethan went to Spain for _a holiday._

I cannot help you since _I have no money._

> These are just examples of sentences with possible reasons. Accept other sentences that are grammatically correct, but make sure a reason is given [e.g. 'Ethan went to Spain for a week.' gives a period of time, not a reason].

Sentence practice

Write a sentence explaining why someone fell over. Use a **preposition** in your answer.

Andrei slipped and fell because of the icy patch on the path.

35

This is an example of a sentence using 'because of' to give a reason for the fall. 'Due to' could also be used in this sentence. There should be a noun phrase after the preposition [e.g. the wet mud by the gate].

Lesson 25 Paragraphs: non-fiction

Focus using paragraphs to organise ideas around a theme

Key terms paragraph

Focus text **Introduction: Many animals live in or close to the river.**
Fish
Amphibians
Birds
Mammals

TEACH

Display the focus text. Explain that this is a plan for a piece of non-fiction writing. Discuss what it tells us about the piece of writing [e.g. What is it about? What aspects of the subject will be covered?]. Invite the pupils to suggest what sort of information might be included under these headings.

Ask the pupils to explain how the writer might use paragraphs when writing this text [e.g. a paragraph on each group of animals]. Ask if they can explain what a paragraph is [a group of sentences about one main idea] and what it looks like on the page [e.g. each new paragraph begins on a new line, often with a small gap separating it from the previous paragraph].

Explain that we use paragraphs in a longer piece of writing to make it easier to follow. We divide a non-fiction text into a series of paragraphs, each focusing on a different aspect of the subject [e.g. in the focus text each paragraph is about a different group of animals]. Each individual paragraph is about one idea; together the paragraphs help to develop the theme of the text.

We start a new paragraph when we start writing about a new idea. The opening sentence of the paragraph introduces the new idea. Invite the pupils to suggest opening sentences for the paragraphs in the focus text [e.g. Many mammals make their home along the riverbank.].

Explain that a plan, as in the focus text, helps us to organise our ideas for each paragraph before we start writing. We decide what aspects of the subject to include and how to order them to develop the theme, with ideas following on in a logical sequence.

EXTEND Look at how to link ideas across paragraphs – for example, using adverbials and pronouns.

PRACTISE

Pupil book page 36

APPLY

- The pupils look at how paragraphs are used in different types of non-fiction texts [e.g. accounts; explanations; arguments]. Ask: When is a new paragraph started? How is the theme developed?
- The pupils make paragraph plans for non-fiction writing. They write a heading or a single sentence to show what each paragraph will be about.
- The pupils research a subject before writing about it. They then use headings, grids or other note-making devices to organise the information and help with paragraph planning.

ASSESS

Dictation: Roads are dangerous places. Children need to know how to stay safe.
Say: Make a plan showing a series of paragraphs to develop this theme.
Answer: Look for paragraphs on different themes [e.g. not playing near roads; crossing roads safely; wearing reflective clothing to be seen].

Pupil book answers

Paragraphs: non-fiction

Remember

Paragraphs are used in a longer piece of writing to make it easier to follow the ideas in it. In non-fiction writing, each paragraph focuses on a different aspect of the subject. A new paragraph indicates a new idea.

Introduction: Many animals live in or close to the river.
Paragraph 1:   Fish
Paragraph 2:   Amphibians
Paragraph 3:   Birds
Paragraph 4:   Mammals

Try it

1 In a piece of writing on the subject 'Wild weather', each **paragraph** focuses on a different type of extreme weather. Write what each paragraph might be about.

Paragraph 1: _Tornadoes_

Paragraph 2: _Hurricanes_

Paragraph 3: _Blizzards_

Paragraph 4: _Droughts_

Paragraph 5: _Electric storms_

These are examples of possible subjects for each paragraph, with each one covering a different aspect of 'wild weather'.

2 Plan a piece of writing on the subject 'How to keep warm'. Write a sentence to show what each **paragraph** will be about.

Paragraph 1: 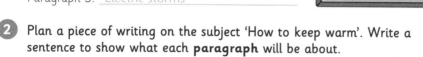 _In cold weather, it is important to wear the right clothes._

Paragraph 2: _Warm food and hot drinks help to keep you warm._

Paragraph 3: _Exercise can help to keep the body warm._

Paragraph 4: _There are many ways of heating our homes._

Paragraph 5: _Insulation helps to keep our houses warm._

This example shows how paragraphs might be used to develop the theme. Each paragraph has a clear focus and the order shows a logical sequence of ideas [e.g. starting with the individual and then looking at homes].

They could be used as the first sentence in a paragraph. Look for some variation in the sentences [e.g. not always 'It is important to ...' or 'We can stay warm by ...']. Discuss possible wording with the pupils.

Sentence practice

Write the text for 'Wild weather' or 'How to keep warm', using **paragraphs** to organise your ideas. Write it on a new piece of paper.

Look for clearly marked paragraphs, with each paragraph developing one key point. Each paragraph should have an opening sentence that introduces the idea, which is then developed with relevant information. The information may be sketchy in places if the pupils are not familiar with the subject.

Lesson 26 Paragraphs: stories

Focus using paragraphs to show the stages in a story

Key terms paragraph, adverbial

Focus text "Don't go playing near the river," said Aunt Olivia, as Arthur headed for the door. It was the summer holidays and Arthur was visiting his aunt. He liked staying at Aunt Olivia's. She lived miles from anywhere and there were so many interesting places to explore. Aunt Olivia let Arthur roam wherever he wanted – apart from the river.

TEACH

Show the focus text. Explain that this is the first paragraph of a story. Read it aloud and discuss how the story might continue. Ask: What will Arthur do? [probably ignore his aunt's warning] Work with the pupils to agree the main events of the story. Record them as a list of short sentences [e.g. Arthur went exploring. He went to play near the river. He got into trouble. He had to be rescued. He went home to his aunt.].

Explain that in stories we use paragraphs to help the reader follow the sequence of events. We start a new paragraph when the story moves on – when the time or place changes, or when a new event or character is introduced. Read through your list of events for the story about Arthur and discuss how the story moves on at each stage [e.g. change of place when he goes exploring; change of time, going to the river; new event when he gets into trouble; new character to rescue him]. Remind the pupils that each stage of the story needs a new paragraph.

Discuss how the time and place is established in the focus text near the start of the opening paragraph. Explain that, similarly, the first sentence of a paragraph should signal how the story has moved on. Remind the pupils that we can use adverbials to do this. Discuss suitable adverbials to introduce each paragraph in the Arthur story [e.g. That morning, Arthur went exploring in the woods. After a few hours, he went to play near the river.].

EXTEND Discuss how to develop ideas within paragraphs [e.g. using more adverbials, and pronouns].

PRACTISE

Pupil book page 37

APPLY

- The pupils write their own version of the 'Arthur' story, following the plan made above and adding details about the events but changing the characters, the setting and the warning.
- The pupils make paragraph plans to show the main stages in various familiar stories. They then use these to invent and write new stories with the same patterns.
- The pupils use adverbials as paragraph prompts to introduce or lead into each paragraph. They could use adverbs [e.g. Later, ...; Much later, ...], prepositional phrases [e.g. In the forest, ...] or clauses [e.g. As the sun was setting, ...].
- The pupils use the same method of planning to write a factual account of an event or a biography.

ASSESS

Dictation: It all started when Dan Simpkins dared me to climb over Mrs Green's garden wall.
Say: Make a paragraph plan to show the sequence of events.
Answer: Look for paragraphs used to show changes in time, place, and plot.

Pupil book answers

Paragraphs: stories

Remember

In stories, **paragraphs** are used to help the reader follow the sequence of events. A new paragraph begins when the story moves on – in time or place, or because of a new event or character. **Adverbials** are often used to show these changes.

Opening: "Don't go playing near the river," said Aunt Olivia, as Arthur headed for the door.

Paragraph 1:   <u>That morning</u>, Arthur went exploring <u>in the woods</u>.

Paragraph 2:   <u>After a few hours</u>, he went to play <u>near the river</u>.

Try it

1 Here is the main sequence of events in a story about three travellers on a quest. Add **adverbials** to show how the story moves on.

<u>Early one morning,</u> the travellers set off <u>on their journey.</u>

<u>For many days,</u> they were lost <u>in a dark forest.</u>

<u>With the help of an owl,</u> they found their way <u>by following a trail.</u>

<u>After weeks of travelling,</u> they met a troll <u>while crossing a river.</u>

<u>After a long struggle,</u> they escaped <u>with the help of a magic fish.</u>

<u>In the end,</u> they found their reward <u>in a secret cave.</u>

2 Make a plan for a story about some children who find a bag of gold coins. Use **adverbials** to show how the story moves on.

<u>While playing on the beach,</u> the children found a bag of gold coins.

<u>Suddenly, a pirate appeared and wanted the coins back.</u>

<u>The children were chased over the clifftop by the pirate.</u>

<u>After a long time, they escaped by tricking the pirate.</u>

<u>When they got home, they returned the coins to the real owner.</u>

Sentence practice

Write one of the two stories above using **paragraphs** to show the sequence of events within it. Write your story on a new piece of paper.

37

This is an example of how adverbials might be used to show time and place or introduce new characters that help or hinder the travellers. Check that commas follow any fronted adverbials. Look for enough detail to build up a clear sequence of events. Compare the pupils' answers.

This is an example of how the story might develop with a problem and resolution. Look for a range of adverbials used to give details about time and place or characters and events. Check for commas after fronted adverbials and see if the pupils have maintained the tense of the first sentence. It is useful to plan stories in the past tense as a reminder to use it when writing.

Look for clearly marked paragraphs that indicate new events and changes of time or place.

Look for the use of adverbials to show time and place in the opening sentences of paragraphs.

Lesson 27   Negative sentences

Focus   forming negative sentences

Key terms   statement, contraction, apostrophe, verb, Standard English

Focus text   I would recommend this car. There is something special about it. Inside, it has enough space for the whole family. There is room in the boot for my shopping.

I wouldn't recommend this car. There is nothing special about it. Inside, it does not have enough space for the whole family. There is no room in the boot for my shopping.

TEACH

Show the first review and read it aloud. Discuss whether it is a positive review or a negative one [positive – it makes positive statements about the car].

Show the second review and read it aloud. Ask: Is this review positive or negative? [negative] Invite the pupils to compare the sentences with those in the first review. Identify and underline the negative words that have changed the meaning of each sentence [–n't, nothing, not, no].

Explain that we can make a positive statement into a negative one by using negative words such as 'no', 'not', 'nothing', 'never' or 'nowhere', or by using the contraction –n't with a verb.

Explain that sometimes we just add the negative word into the sentence [e.g. there is room/there is <u>no</u> room], or we add the contraction –n't to a verb in the sentence [e.g. I would/I would<u>n't</u>]. Sometimes, we swap a word for a negative one [e.g. something special/<u>nothing</u> special]. Other times, we need to add an extra verb to go with the negative word [e.g. it has enough space/it <u>does not</u> have enough space].

Invite the pupils to suggest some more positive/negative sentences about the car [e.g. There is a sunroof./ There is no sunroof.]. Explain that we must only use *one* negative word in a sentence. If there are two negative words, they cancel each other out [e.g. It doesn't have no sunroof.].

You may wish to revise contractions involving verbs and the word 'not'. Remind the pupils that the apostrophe marks the missing letter 'o' in 'not' [e.g. can't; don't; doesn't; couldn't; wouldn't].

EXTEND   Discuss double negatives that sometimes occur in spoken language [e.g. I haven't done nothing!]. Explain that these are not Standard English.

PRACTISE

Pupil book page 38

APPLY

- The pupils write reviews of books and films, using positive and negative statements.
- The pupils write adverts using negative statements as well as positive ones [e.g. Our new tangle-free shampoo is marvellous. You will never need a hairbrush again.].
- When writing arguments for and against, the pupils use both positive and negative statements to weigh up the different opinions.
- The pupils write warnings using negative words [e.g. Never look directly at the sun.].

ASSESS

Dictation: Jonas is always late. He is <u>never</u> on time. He <u>doesn't</u> have an alarm clock.
Say: Underline the two negative words.

Pupil book answers

Negative sentences

Remember

You can make a **positive** statement into a **negative** one by using negative words such as 'no', 'not', 'nothing', 'never' or 'nowhere', or by adding the contraction **–n't** to a verb.

I would recommend this car.   I wouldn't recommend this car.
There is enough space.   There is not enough space.
There is something special about it. There is nothing special about it.

Try it

1. Underline the **negative** word that changes the meaning of the sentence.

   The men were <u>not</u> digging a hole in the road.

   I knew <u>nothing</u> about the stolen painting.

   We <u>never</u> do the shopping on Friday.

   There is <u>no</u> room in the suitcase.

   People <u>don't</u> care about the park.

   The stray cat had <u>nowhere</u> to go.

2. Rewrite the **positive** statement as a **negative** statement.

   We have food in the fridge.   We have no food in the fridge.

   They have something to give you.   They have nothing to give you.

   Fatima has been to France.   Fatima has never been to France.

   I will wait for you.   I will not wait for you.

   You have seen this film before.   You haven't seen this film before.

   She could hear his voice.   She couldn't hear his voice.

Sentence practice

Write <u>one</u> **positive** statement and <u>one</u> **negative** statement about a football match.

There were no goals in the first half.

There were goals in the second half.

There are other ways of making the statements into negative sentences [e.g. We do not have food in the fridge.], but check that there are no double negatives [e.g. We don't have <u>no</u> food in the fridge.].

Contractions should be spelt correctly with a correctly placed apostrophe.

These are just examples of positive and negative statements.

Contractions must be spelt correctly with a correctly placed apostrophe.

Lesson 28 Questions and question tags

Focus grammatical patterns in questions; using question tags

Key terms question, statement, command, question mark, **question tag**, comma

Focus text **Hattie:**   Who will help me bake a cherry pie.
Cara: Not I. Ask Dora if she will help.
Hattie: Dora, will you help me bake a cherry pie.
Dora: Not I. You could ask Marlon if he will help.
Hattie: You will help me, won't you.
Marlon: Not I. Do it yourself.

TEACH

Show the focus text. Read the script aloud. Ask the pupils if the story sounds familiar.

Discuss which sentences should end with a question mark rather than a full stop. Write in question marks at the end of lines 1, 3 and 5. Discuss how the pupils knew these sentences were questions [e.g. they ask something; they need a response; they begin with a question word].

Discuss the characters' responses to the question. Which are statements and which are commands? Recap differences between statements and commands [e.g. commands are direct; they often start with the verb; they have no subject – because they are directed at the subject].

Explain that there are three main ways of forming questions. The pupils should already be familiar with forming questions using question words [e.g. Who will help me ...?] and by reordering the subject and verb at the beginning of a statement [e.g. You will .../Will you ...?].

The third question in the focus text introduces the use of question tags. Underline the question tag [You will help me, won't you?]. Explain that a question tag is a phrase added to the end of a statement to turn it into a question. Adding the question tag invites a response. Explain that when we add a question tag, a comma is used to separate it from the original statement.

Make some statements [e.g. You do like cherry pie.] and invite the pupils to add the appropriate question tags [e.g. don't you?].

EXTEND Explore with the pupils how the main clause shows whether a sentence is a statement, question or command [e.g. After tea, ask Dora to help. Cara, can you help?].

PRACTISE

Pupil book page 39

APPLY

- The pupils orally rehearse and then write a script using different types of sentence, including questions with question tags [e.g. We've been here before, haven't we?].
- The pupils use questions with question tags in letters to invite the reader to respond [e.g. You will send me a picture, won't you?].
- The pupils use question tags when writing adverts [e.g. You want the best trainers, don't you?].
- In stories, the pupils use question tags in direct speech to introduce events [e.g. "That's Joe, isn't it?"].

ASSESS

Dictation: How much further? We're nearly there, aren't we? Is that the sea over there?
Say: Underline the question tag.
Check: All punctuation is correct, including the comma and apostrophes.

Pupil book answers

Questions and question tags

Remember

A **question tag** is a phrase added to the end of a **statement** to turn it into a **question**. Adding the question tag invites the listener or reader to respond or give an answer. A **comma** is used to separate the question tag from the statement.

You will help me, <u>won't you?</u>

Try it

1 Underline the **question tag** that makes the statement into a question.

You can come to the library, <u>can't you?</u>

This is the song you wanted, <u>isn't it?</u>

You have been bowling, <u>haven't you?</u>

You won first prize, <u>didn't you?</u>

We should be home by now, <u>shouldn't we?</u>

The concert was brilliant, <u>wasn't it?</u>

2 Add a **question tag** to make each statement into a question. Use the correct punctuation.

We can go swimming on Friday <u>, can't we?</u>

He owns an Alsatian dog <u>, doesn't he?</u>

I did write back <u>, didn't I?</u>

That singer was amazing <u>, wasn't she?</u>

You do like fishing <u>, don't you?</u>

Chocolate-chip cookies are your favourite <u>, aren't they?</u>

Sentence practice

Write <u>two</u> **questions** to ask a new classmate. Use **question tags**.

Your name's Ross, isn't it? You live in Park Street, don't you?

39

Encourage the pupils to read the sentences aloud so that they become familiar with the form of question tags.

The question tag must be correctly punctuated with a comma separating it from the original statement, a correctly placed apostrophe and a question mark.

Question tags are often used quite naturally in spoken English, so the pupils may find it useful to say the sentences aloud.

These are just examples of possible questions. The question tag must be correctly punctuated with a comma separating it from the original statement, a correctly placed apostrophe and a question mark.

Lesson 29 Adjectives with prefixes and suffixes

Focus forming adjectives using prefixes and suffixes

Key terms adjective, root word, prefix, suffix

Focus text Outside, it looked like an unremarkable wooden chest but inside there were so many magical things: expensive furs, glorious silks, valuable jewels, glittering ornaments, delightful trinkets ... so many irreplaceable treasures.

TEACH

Show the focus text and read it aloud. Discuss what the chest is like on the outside and how it is different on the inside. Discuss the highlighted words and what they tell us about the items.

Ask: What type of word is highlighted? [adjectives] Ask the pupils what they notice about these adjectives [e.g. they are formed with suffixes and sometimes prefixes].

Explain that lots of adjectives are formed by adding suffixes to root words. Underline the suffixes used in the focus text [–able, –en, –al, –ive, –ous, –ing, –ful]. As you do this, remind the pupils that sometimes the spelling of the root word changes when a suffix is added – for example, losing the letter 'e' when adding a vowel suffix [expense/expensive], or changing 'y' to 'i' [glory/glorious].

Ask the pupils to suggest other adjectives ending with these and other suffixes [e.g. –y, –less] that could be used to describe treasures [e.g. impressive; gleaming; shiny; wonderful; beautiful].

Discuss the words in the focus text that also have prefixes [unremarkable, irreplaceable]. Circle the prefixes [un–, ir–] and discuss how they change the meaning of the adjective [they make it mean the opposite].

EXTEND Discuss other prefixes that make adjectives mean the opposite [e.g. in–; im–; dis–].

PRACTISE

Pupil book page 40

APPLY

- The pupils write adverts for amazing products using adjectives formed with prefixes and/or suffixes [e.g. unbelievable; unmissable; attractive; wonderful].
- Together, collect adjectives to describe story characters [e.g. bashful; ruthless; heroic; carefree; dishonest]. Encourage the pupils to use these words when planning and writing their own stories.
- When the pupils are reading, encourage them to identify adjectives formed with suffixes and build up lists of useful words. They should use dictionaries to check the spelling and meaning of adjectives.
- In other subject areas, encourage the pupils to look for adjectives with suffixes [e.g. rectangular; hexagonal; European].

ASSESS

Dictation: The foolish man made a dreadful mistake when he left his comfortable little house to live in a massive mansion.

Say: Underline the adjectives formed by adding suffixes. Add another sentence using an adjective formed from the word 'expense'.

Answer: e.g. The mansion was expensive to run.

Pupil book answers

Adjectives with prefixes and suffixes

Remember

Many **adjectives** are formed by adding a **suffix** to a **root word**.

delightful   expensive   valuable

magical   glorious   glittering

You can also add a **prefix** to an adjective. This changes its meaning.

irreplaceable   unremarkable

Try it

1 Add a **suffix** to each word to make it into an **adjective**.

sensation	sensational	beauty	beautiful
attract	attractive	chat	chatty
danger	dangerous	entertain	entertaining
thought	thoughtless	create	creative
child	childish	believe	believable
gold	golden	history	historic

2 Complete each sentence with an **adjective** formed from the word next to it.

We are often told to avoid eating __unhealthy__ foods such as sweets.   (health)

I think I may have made a __dreadful__ mistake.   (dread)

The watch did not cost a lot. It was __inexpensive__ .   (expense)

He is a rude and __disagreeable__ person.   (agree)

She was __nervous__ before she went on stage.   (nerve)

I knew I was in trouble when I saw Mum's __disapproving__ look.   (approve)

Sentence practice

Write a sentence using <u>two</u> **adjectives**, one formed from the word 'poison' and one from the word 'magic'.

The villain's magical potion was extremely poisonous.

40

The adjectives should be spelt correctly, including those that require a change in the spelling of the root word.

Accept other adjectives to those shown [e.g. childlike; thoughtful] but do not accept words that are not adjectives [e.g. entertainment].

The adjectives should be spelt correctly, including those that require a change in the spelling of the root word.

Some of the adjectives need a prefix as well as a suffix. The context of the sentence shows when a prefix is needed to make an adjective with the opposite meaning, so make sure the pupils read the complete sentence.

This is just an example of a sentence using the two adjectives.

Lesson 30 Word families

Focus word families based on common roots and root words related by meaning

Key terms word family, root word, **root**

Focus text There are various different types of geranium. They come in a varied range of colours. Some varieties show variation in the leaves.

multitude	manufacture	multi-coloured
manicure	manuscript	multiply

TEACH

Show the first part of the focus text and read it aloud. Ask the pupils to identify words from the same word family [various, varied, varieties, variation]. Underline the words and discuss their meanings. Discuss what common root word they share [vary].

Show the second part of the focus text. Ask the pupils to sort the words into two word families using clues in the form and meanings of the words [multitude, multi-coloured, multiply; manufacture, manicure, manuscript]. Discuss how they know.

Explain that words belonging to the same word family are related in how they are formed and in their meaning. The words may have the same root word [e.g. vary], part of a word such as a prefix [e.g. multi–] or a common 'root' that is not a recognisable word [e.g. manu/mani].

Discuss the related meanings of the words in the 'vary' word family. They all have meanings related to varying, changing, being different. Explain that the origin of these words is a Latin word meaning 'to change'. Ask the pupils to name other words in this word family and discuss how this meaning relates to them [e.g. variable; variegated].

Discuss the meaning of the words in the other two word families. Ask the pupils if they can work out the meaning of the prefix 'multi–' [many]. Discuss other words in this family [e.g. multiple; multiplex]. Explain that the origin of the 'manu/mani' word family is a Latin word meaning 'hand'. Discuss how this meaning relates to the words [e.g. 'manuscript' – written by hand; 'manufacture' – made by hand].

EXTEND Challenge the pupils to use dictionaries to find more words in these word families [e.g. manual].

PRACTISE

Pupil book page 41

APPLY

- Encourage the pupils to use their knowledge of root words to work out the meaning of new words they meet when they are reading.
- In other subjects, invite the pupils to look for words that belong in the same word family [e.g. technology, technique].
- The pupils use dictionary entries to find words belonging in the same word family and to create word family trees.

ASSESS

Dictation: We are searching the local area to find a good location for our new swimming pool.
Say: Underline the two words in this sentence that belong in the same word family. Both words come from a root meaning 'place'. Can you think of another word in the same family?
Answer: e.g. relocate; locality

Pupil book answers

Word families

Remember

A **word family** is a group of words that share the same **root word** or 'root'. All the words in a word family have meanings related to this shared root.

| vary | variety | various | variable | (meaning: to change) |
| multi– | multitude | multi-coloured | multiply | (meaning: many) |

Try it

1 Draw lines to match <u>two</u> words in the same **word family** with the meaning of their **root**.

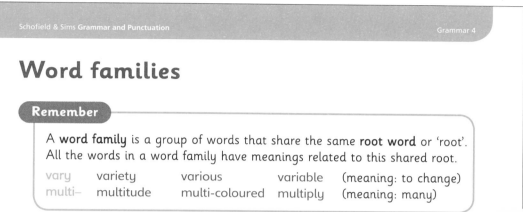

structure
service
fraction
attract
pedal
magnificent

pedestrian
magnify
tractor
construct
fracture
servant

(root meaning: to pull)
(root meaning: to break)
(root meaning: foot)
(root meaning: great)
(root meaning: slave)
(root meaning: build)

You could discuss the meanings of the words and how they relate to the root, or discuss other words belonging to the same word family [e.g. 'restructure' or 'destruction' for the 'struct' family].

2 Decide what the underlined **root** means in the **word families** below. Choose and write a meaning from the box.

> end   to say   one   to look   ten   to write

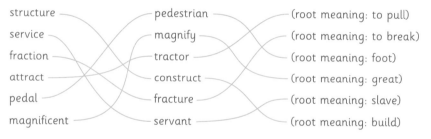

<u>spect</u>ator	spectacle	inspect	spectacular	to look
<u>dict</u>ate	dictation	dictator	edict	to say
<u>dec</u>imal	decade	decathlon	decimetre	ten
<u>fin</u>al	finish	finale	definite	end
<u>uni</u>que	unicorn	unite	unit	one
<u>scrib</u>ble	describe	scripture	manuscript	to write

Ask the pupils to explain how they worked out the meaning of the root. What shared meaning did they find between the words in the word family?

Sentence practice

Write a sentence using <u>two</u> words with the **root word** 'medic'.

I went to the medical centre to get some medicine.

This is just an example. Accept any sentence that makes sense and is punctuated correctly.

41

Revision 3 answers

This page revises punctuation introduced in this book. Encourage the pupils to proofread their writing to check that this punctuation is used correctly. The focus of each activity is given to help identify areas that may need further reinforcement.

Focus: commas after fronted adverbials

Remind the pupils that a comma is needed after a fronted adverbial – this can be an adverb, phrase or clause.

Focus: inverted commas and other punctuation to indicate direct speech

Check that all punctuation is used correctly, including the comma after 'Emma replied'.

Focus: apostrophes to mark singular/ plural possession; distinguishing plural –s and possessive –'s

Remind the pupils to check that (1) it shows possession – does something belong to the noun?; and (2) if so, does the word before the apostrophe show the 'owner' or 'owners'?

Grammar 4   Schofield & Sims **Grammar and Punctuation**

Revision 3

1 Add a **comma** in the correct place in each sentence.

Happily, the man whistled as he walked along.

Just after sunrise, the little ship left the harbour.

While we were talking, Alex slipped out of the room.

With a fearful cry, the pirates attacked.

2 Write the sentences in the speech bubbles as **direct speech**. Punctuate your answer correctly.

Are you hungry?

I'm starving.

"Are you hungry?"   Freddie asked Emma.

Emma replied , "I'm starving."

3 Rewrite each sentence, using an **apostrophe** correctly.

The childrens' names are on their folders.
    The children's names are on their folders.

The cats whisker's began to twitch.
    The cat's whiskers began to twitch.

The girls ate all Marthas' cakes.
    The girls ate all Martha's cakes.

The ladie's hats were very colourful.
    The ladies' hats were very colourful.

4 Add the correct **punctuation mark** to the end of the sentence.

You will come to my party, won't you ?

Now explain why there is a **comma** in the sentence above.

    The comma separates the question tag from the rest of the sentence.

42

Focus: recognising questions using question tags

Answers should refer to the question tag and/or explain that the comma separates the question tag from the rest of the sentence.

This page revises terminology introduced in this book and reinforces earlier work on different sentence types, focusing on commands.

The focus of each activity is given to help identify terms and concepts that may need further reinforcement.

Schofield & Sims **Grammar and Punctuation**   Grammar 4

5 Underline the **co-ordinating conjunctions** in these sentences.

I must be ill because I feel shivery <u>and</u> I have a headache.

After we finished tea, I could play in my room <u>or</u> watch television until bedtime.

I like strawberry <u>and</u> orange flavoured sweets <u>but</u> I don't like lemon <u>or</u> lime.

When he took the penalty, he struck the ball hard <u>but</u> it missed the goal <u>and</u> went into the crowd.

I liked the shirt <u>but</u> it was too big for me when I tried it on.

Focus: co-ordinating conjunctions

Only the words 'and', 'but' and 'or' should be underlined. Other conjunctions [because, after, when] are subordinating conjunctions.

6 Rewrite each sentence using the **Standard English** form of the **verb**.

We was going for a walk.   We were going for a walk.

I done the washing up.   I did the washing up.

My handwriting ain't that bad. My handwriting isn't that bad.

She knowed the answer.   She knew the answer.

He teached me how to dive.   He taught me how to dive.

Focus: Standard English verb forms

Remind the pupils to always check that they use Standard English verb forms in their writing.

7 Complete each sentence with a **possessive pronoun**.

These are your shoes and those are _____mine_____.

The red car is _____ours_____.

That rugby shirt must be _____hers_____.

This model spaceship is _____theirs_____.

That cap is _____his_____.

This sandwich is _____yours_____.

Focus: possessive pronouns

The pupils can use any suitable pronoun [mine, yours, his, hers, ours, theirs]. However, do not accept a possessive determiner with a noun [e.g. my shoes] or a possessive noun [e.g. Sam's].

8 Complete each sentence so that it is a **command**.

After you've finished, tidy your things away.

Before you go shopping, make a list of the things you need.

Once the pizza is cooked, cut it into pieces.

Carefully, put the hamster back in its cage.

If you feel unwell, tell an adult straightaway.

When you have finished, check your answers.

43

Focus: grammatical patterns of commands

These are just examples of possible main clauses in the form of commands that follow on from the given fronted adverbials. Check that the pupils' answers are commands, beginning with an imperative verb [e.g. tidy ...; make ...].

Writing task 3: Analysis sheet

Tick the circles to show amount of evidence found in writing:

1 No evidence
2 Some evidence
3 Clear evidence

Pupil name: _____

Date: _____

Assessing punctuation

The writing sample demonstrates:	Evidence		
sentence boundaries demarcated with capital letters and appropriate end punctuation.	1	2	3
capital letters used for 'I' and proper nouns.	1	2	3
commas used to separate items in a list.	1	2	3
apostrophes used correctly in contracted forms or for singular and plural possession [e.g. most people's bikes].	1	2	3
inverted commas and other punctuation marks used correctly to indicate direct speech.	1	2	3
commas used after fronted adverbials and before question tags [e.g. You ..., don't you?].	1	2	3

Assessing grammar and sentence structure

The writing sample demonstrates:	Evidence		
grammatically correct sentences [e.g. Standard English verb forms; agreement].	1	2	3
a variety of sentence types [statements, commands, exclamations, questions – including question tags].	1	2	3
sentences with more than one clause, using co-ordinating conjunctions and a range of subordinating conjunctions.	1	2	3
the correct use of tense with some perfect forms [e.g. I have invented ...; It has been tested ...].	1	2	3
the accurate use of pronouns to avoid repetition and build cohesion [e.g. It could be yours!].	1	2	3
adverbials to add detail about where, when, why, how [e.g. on the handlebars; due to rain], and to vary sentence openings.	1	2	3
expanded noun phrases to describe and add detail.	1	2	3

Key target: _____

Writing task 3: Pupil checklist

Name: _____   Date: _____

Reread what you have written to check that it makes sense. Tick the circle if you have correctly used the punctuation or grammar feature in your writing.

Punctuation

◯ I have used capital letters and full stops to punctuate sentences.

◯ I have used question marks or exclamation marks where needed (e.g. It looks great, doesn't it?).

◯ I have used capital letters for 'I' and any names.

◯ I have used commas to separate items in a list.

◯ I have used apostrophes in contractions (e.g. it isn't) and for possession (e.g. Ian's bike).

◯ I have used inverted commas and other punctuation in direct speech.

◯ I have used commas after fronted adverbials.

Grammar and sentences

◯ I have written in sentences and used Standard English verb forms.

◯ I have used different sentence types (e.g. questions, exclamations, commands).

◯ I have used sentences with more than one clause, and with co-ordinating and subordinating conjunctions.

◯ I have used tense correctly.

◯ I have used pronouns to avoid repetition and their meaning is clear.

◯ I have used adverbials to add detail about events – where, when, how or why.

◯ I have used longer noun phrases to describe and give details.

◯ I have used different sentence starters (e.g. adverbs, prepositional phrases).

Teacher feedback

My key target: _____
_____

Final test

Name: _____

1 Complete the sentence with a **preposition**.

On my birthday, I saw a pile of colourful presents _____ the kitchen table.

1 mark

2 Rewrite this sentence in the **present tense**.

I could tell by her face that she was unhappy.

_____

1 mark

3 Tick the sentences that must end with a **question mark**.

What a brilliant song ☐

What is this song ☐

Have you heard this song before ☐

I really like this song ☐

This is a great song, isn't it ☐

1 mark

4 Tick the correct box to show whether the underlined word is a **noun** or a **verb**.

Sentence	Noun	Verb
I always keep a <u>promise</u>.		
Soldiers <u>guard</u> the gates of the palace.		
We <u>exercise</u> every morning.		
The tour <u>guide</u> showed me the way.		

1 mark

5 Complete the sentence below using the correct **pronouns**.

Vikesh and I were looking for Isabel but _____
could not find _____ .

1 mark

6 Write the **plural** form of each **noun** to complete these collective nouns.

a herd of _____ (giraffe)

a swarm of _____ (fly)

a gang of _____ (thief)

a flock of _____ (sheep)

a class of _____ (child)

1 mark

7 Complete this **noun phrase** with an **adjective** formed from the word 'fame'.

a _____ singer

1 mark

8 Write a sentence using the word 'late' as an **adverb**.

_____

1 mark

9 Add a **prefix** to each **adjective** to make it mean the opposite.

The answer was _____correct.

The man was _____honest.

The task was _____possible.

_____pleasant smells drifted from the kitchen.

1 mark

10 Underline the **adverbial** in each of the sentences below.

The river burst its banks around midnight.

Nearby, people found their homes were flooded.

Our carpets were ruined in the flood.

1 mark

11 Underline the **co-ordinating conjunction** in the sentence below.

Mr O'Neill was strict but he was always fair.

1 mark

12 Underline all the **determiners** in the sentence below.

The elephant has two tusks and a long trunk.

1 mark

13 Insert a **comma** in the correct place in this sentence.

Early on Sunday morning he began to paint the house.

1 mark

14 Tick <u>one</u> box to show which word is a **possessive pronoun**.

<u>You</u> must write <u>Robbie's</u> address below <u>mine</u> in <u>your</u> address book.

☐   ☐   ☐   ☐

1 mark

15 Rewrite these sentences as **direct speech**.

Would you like to come to my party asked Lauren.

_____

Molly smiled and said that would be lovely.

_____

1 mark

16 Tick <u>one</u> box to show how the underlined words are used in the sentence.

Last week, I took some old clothes to <u>the charity shop in the town centre</u>.

adverbial ☐   noun phrase ☐

subordinate clause ☐   main clause ☐

☐

1 mark

17 The sentence below uses an **apostrophe** incorrectly. Explain why.

He's helping Dad to clean the window's at the back of the house.

_____

_____

☐

1 mark

18 Complete each sentence, using a **Standard English verb form**.

We _____ wearing shorts and T-shirts.   (am was were)

I have _____ to Mr Robson.   (spoken speak spoke)

I ate my breakfast and _____ my juice.   (drinked drank drunk)

☐

1 mark

19 Rewrite the sentence below adding an **adverbial** to the start of the sentence. Remember to punctuate your answer correctly.

A wolf began to howl.

_____

☐

1 mark

20 Insert an **apostrophe** in the correct place in this sentence.

All the babies pushchairs were left outside.

☐

1 mark

End of test

Final test: Mark scheme

Q	Focus	Answer
1	prepositions in noun phrases	**Award 1 mark** for any preposition that makes sense [e.g. under; behind]. On my birthday, I saw a pile of colourful presents <u>on</u> the kitchen table.
2	simple present tense	**Award 1 mark** for <u>both</u> correct present tense verbs. I <u>can</u> tell by her face that she <u>is</u> unhappy.
3	grammatical patterns in questions, including question tags; question marks	**Award 1 mark** for all <u>three</u> boxes correctly ticked. What is this song ✓ Have you heard this song before ✓ This is a great song, isn't it ✓
4	nouns and verbs	**Award 1 mark** for all <u>four</u> correct.

Sentence	Noun	Verb
I always keep a <u>promise</u>.	✓	
Soldiers <u>guard</u> the gates of the palace.		✓
We <u>exercise</u> every morning.		✓
The tour <u>guide</u> showed me the way.	✓	

Q	Focus	Answer
5	appropriate choice of pronoun within sentences	**Award 1 mark** for <u>both</u> pronouns correct. Vikesh and I were looking for Isabel but <u>we</u> could not find <u>her</u>.
6	plurals: regular and irregular	**Award 1 mark** for all <u>five</u> plural nouns spelt correctly. a herd of <u>giraffes</u> a swarm of <u>flies</u> a gang of <u>thieves</u> a flock of <u>sheep</u> a class of <u>children</u>
7	forming adjectives using suffixes	**Award 1 mark** for the adjective spelt correctly. a <u>famous</u> singer
8	adverbs	**Award 1 mark** for any sentence that correctly uses the word 'late' as an adverb, e.g. He arrived <u>late</u> for the party. He came to school <u>late</u>. *Do not accept* 'late' used as an adjective, e.g. 'I was late.'; 'He was late.'
9	using prefixes to change the meaning of adjectives	**Award 1 mark** for all <u>four</u> correct prefixes. The answer was <u>in</u>correct. The man was <u>dis</u>honest. The task was <u>im</u>possible. <u>Un</u>pleasant smells drifted from the kitchen.

10	adverbials	**Award 1 mark** for all <u>three</u> adverbials correctly underlined.
		The river burst its banks <u>around midnight</u>.
		<u>Nearby</u>, people found their homes were flooded.
		Our carpets were ruined <u>in the flood</u>.
11	co-ordinating conjunctions	**Award 1 mark** for the co-ordinating conjunction 'but' correctly underlined.
		Mr O'Neill was strict <u>but</u> he was always fair.
12	determiners	**Award 1 mark** for all <u>three</u> determiners correctly underlined.
		<u>The</u> elephant has <u>two</u> tusks and <u>a</u> long trunk.
13	commas after fronted adverbials	**Award 1 mark** for a correctly placed comma.
		Early on Sunday morning, he began to paint the house.
14	possessive pronouns	**Award 1 mark** for the correct box ticked.
		mine ✓
15	inverted commas and other punctuation to indicate direct speech	**Award 1 mark** for <u>both</u> correctly punctuated sentences.
		"Would you like to come to my party?" asked Lauren.
		Molly smiled and said, "That would be lovely."
16	expanded noun phrases	**Award 1 mark** for the correct box ticked.
		noun phrase ✓
17	apostrophes: difference between plural –s and possessive –'s	**Award 1 mark** for a suitable explanation referring to the apostrophe added to the plural –s in the word 'windows'.
		There should not be an apostrophe in 'windows' because it is a plural/it does not show possession.
		Do not accept answers that do not give a clear explanation, e.g. 'because there is more than one window'
18	Standard English verb forms	**Award 1 mark** for all <u>three</u> correctly chosen verbs.
		We <u>were</u> wearing shorts and T-shirts.
		I have <u>spoken</u> to Mr Robson.
		I ate my breakfast and <u>drank</u> my juice.
19	fronted adverbials; commas after fronted adverbials	**Award 1 mark** for any grammatically correct sentence with a fronted adverbial followed by a comma, e.g.
		<u>In the forest</u>, a wolf began to howl.
		The sentence must also start with a capital letter and end with a full stop.
20	apostrophes to mark plural possession	**Award 1 mark** for <u>one</u> correctly placed apostrophe.
		All the babies' pushchairs were left outside.

Final test: Analysis sheet

Tick the box for each correct answer.

Q	Focus	Pupil names									
1	prepositions in noun phrases										
2	simple present tense										
3	grammatical patterns in questions, including question tags; question marks										
4	nouns and verbs										
5	appropriate choice of pronoun within sentences										
6	plurals: regular and irregular										
7	forming adjectives using suffixes										
8	adverbs										
9	using prefixes to change the meaning of adjectives										
10	adverbials										
11	co-ordinating conjunctions										
12	determiners										
13	commas after fronted adverbials										
14	possessive pronouns										
15	inverted commas and other punctuation to indicate direct speech										
16	expanded noun phrases										
17	apostrophes: difference between plural –s and possessive –'s										
18	Standard English verb forms										
19	fronted adverbials; commas after fronted adverbials										
20	apostrophes to mark plural possession										
	Total correct answers per pupil										

Target tracking sheet

Group: _____

Target: _____

Date: _____ Date for review: _____

Tick the circles to show depth of understanding:
1 Just beginning
2 Progressing
3 Learning is embedded

Pupil name	Evidence from independent writing	Progress in independent writing
		① ② ③
		① ② ③
		① ② ③
		① ② ③
		① ② ③
		① ② ③
		① ② ③
		① ② ③
		① ② ③
		① ② ③

Learning pathways sheet

Pupil name: _____

Date last updated: _____

Tick the circles to show depth of understanding:
1 Just beginning
2 Progressing
3 Learning is embedded

Punctuation pathway

Demarcate sentences with capital letters, full stops, question marks and exclamation marks.
(1) (2) (3)

Use capital letters for 'I' and proper nouns.
(1) (2) (3)

Use commas to separate items in a list.
(1) (2) (3)

Use apostrophes in contractions.
(1) (2) (3)

Use apostrophes for singular and plural possession, but not with plural −s.
(1) (2) (3)

Use inverted commas and other punctuation to indicate direct speech.
(1) (2) (3)

Use commas after fronted adverbials.
(1) (2) (3)

Use commas before question tags.
(1) (2) (3)

Grammar and sentence pathway

Write grammatically correct sentences, using Standard English verbs.
(1) (2) (3)

Vary sentence forms as appropriate: command, question, exclamation, statement.
(1) (2) (3)

Use tense accurately, including progressive and perfect forms.
(1) (2) (3)

Use conjunctions to write sentences with more than one clause.
(1) (2) (3)

Use expanded noun phrases to add detail, using adjectives and prepositional phrases.
(1) (2) (3)

Use adverbials to add detail about where, when, how and why.
(1) (2) (3)

Use pronouns accurately and consistently to avoid repetition.
(1) (2) (3)

Vary sentence openings by fronting adverbials.
(1) (2) (3)

Glossary

Adjective

An **adjective** is a word used to modify or specify a noun [e.g. an angry man; the red car; a beautiful day]. Lesson 5

- **Comparative** and **superlative adjectives** are used to compare nouns. The suffixes −er and −est are added to shorter adjectives [e.g. the faster car; the fastest car]. The words 'more' and 'most' are used with longer adjectives [e.g. a more expensive car; the most expensive car].
- Some adjectives are formed by adding a suffix to a word [e.g. careful; careless].
- Some adjectives are formed by adding both a suffix and a prefix to a word [e.g. unremarkable].
  Lesson 29

Adverb

An **adverb** is a word that modifies a verb or action in a sentence. An adverb can specify *how, where,* or *when* the action took place [e.g. He arrived quietly. He arrived outside. He arrived yesterday.]. Lesson 1

- Sometimes adverbs modify other words, such as another adverb [e.g. really quickly] or an adjective [e.g. a really good idea]. Grammar 5
- Some adverbs are used to show links between ideas or events [e.g. 'meanwhile' shows a time link; 'therefore' shows the result of an action]. Lesson 24
- Some adverbs are used to show how likely or possible an event is [e.g. 'surely' – very likely; 'perhaps' – a possibility]. Grammar 5
- Some adverbs comment on a whole sentence or clause [e.g. Fortunately, the rain stopped.].
  Grammar 5

Adverbial

An **adverbial** is a word, phrase or clause that is used like an adverb – it adds more detail about a verb or event in a sentence. Adverbs can be used as adverbials, as can phrases, including prepositional phrases [e.g. He arrived in the morning. He arrived at the gate. He arrived in a hurry.] or noun phrases [e.g. He arrived last night.]. Lesson 11 Subordinate clauses starting with conjunctions can also be adverbials [e.g. He arrived after I left.]. Lesson 14

- **Fronted adverbials** are adverbial words, phrases or clauses used at the start of a sentence [e.g. Suddenly, the ghost appeared. In the morning, I lay in bed. As the sun was rising, I was still sleeping.]. Commas are always used after fronted adverbials to separate them from the rest of the sentence. Lessons 12, 13 and 14

Apostrophe

An **apostrophe** ['] is a punctuation mark with two different uses:

- it shows the position of missing letters in **contractions** or shortened forms of words that are often used in informal speech [e.g. can't; who's; we've].
- it is used with the letter 's' to show **possession** in the possessive form of nouns [e.g. Sam's hat; both boys' coats; the children's shoes]. Lesson 16
- If the noun is plural and already ends in −s, the apostrophe is added by itself, after the −s [e.g. the parents' meeting]. For irregular plurals not ending in −s, an apostrophe and an 's' are added [e.g. children's playground]. Lessons 17 and 18

Clause

A **clause** is a group of words that are connected together and include a verb. A clause can be a complete sentence or part of a sentence.

- A **main clause** is a clause that makes sense on its own and so could be a sentence in itself [e.g. The little girl shouted.]. A sentence always contains at least one main clause. It can contain more than one clause if the clauses are linked with a co-ordinating conjunction [e.g. The little girl shouted <u>and</u> then she ran away.]. Lessons 1, 2 and 23
- A **subordinate clause** is a less important clause that is added to a main clause, usually using a subordinating conjunction. Lesson 23 It adds extra detail to the main clause [e.g. The little girl shouted <u>when she saw the wolf</u>.]. The subordinate clause 'when she saw the wolf' does not make sense without the main clause. Lessons 2 and 14

Comma

A **comma [,]** is a punctuation mark used to separate different parts of a sentence, for example:

- to separate the items in a list [e.g. She put the fresh eggs, a packet of cheese and some butter in the basket.].
- to separate spoken words from non-spoken words in direct speech [e.g. "I'm hungry," he said.]. Lessons 7 and 8
- to separate a fronted adverbial from the rest of the sentence [e.g. In the forest, the wolf was waiting.]. Lessons 13 and 14

Conjunction

A **conjunction** is a word that joins two words, phrases or clauses together. Conjunctions show how ideas link together [e.g. 'because' shows cause; 'when', 'while', 'until' show time links; 'but', 'although' show contrast].

There are two types of conjunction:

- **Co-ordinating conjunctions** [and, but, or] link together two words, phrases or clauses that are equally important [e.g. Bill <u>and</u> Diane were looking for a house <u>or</u> a flat. Bill preferred a house <u>but</u> Diane wanted a flat.]. Lesson 23
- **Subordinating conjunctions** [e.g. although; as; because; once; until; when; while] introduce a subordinate or less important clause [e.g. Bill preferred to live in a house <u>because</u> he wanted a garden.]. Lessons 2, 14 and 23

Determiner

A **determiner** is the word that is used before a noun [e.g. <u>a</u> cat; <u>this</u> dog]. In a noun phrase, the determiner comes before any adjectives [e.g. <u>a</u> little cat; <u>this</u> big dog]. It helps to specify the noun as known [e.g. <u>my</u> school; <u>this</u> school] or unknown [e.g. <u>a</u> school; <u>some</u> schools]. Lesson 4

- **Articles** ['the', 'a' and 'an'] are the most common determiners. 'The' is the definite article. It shows that the noun that it precedes is known [e.g. <u>the</u> dog]. 'A' or 'an' are indefinite articles. They show that the noun that they precede is unknown [e.g. <u>a</u> cat; <u>an</u> elephant]. 'An' is used before a word beginning with a vowel sound. Lesson 4
- Many other words can also be used as determiners, including demonstratives [e.g. <u>this</u> school], possessives [e.g. <u>your</u> school] and quantifiers [e.g. <u>some</u> schools]. Some of these words can also be used in other ways [e.g. as pronouns] but they are determiners when they are followed by a noun or noun phrase. Lesson 4

Direct speech

Direct speech is when we record what someone says using the speaker's original words. Lessons 7 and 8
- **Inverted commas**, sometimes called **speech marks**, are used to mark the beginning and end of the spoken words [e.g. "My name is Jack."]. Lessons 7 and 8
- Direct speech is often followed by a **reporting clause** [unspoken words that say who is speaking]. A comma is placed within the inverted commas at the end of the spoken words [e.g. "My name is Jack," said the boy.] Lessons 7 and 8
- If the spoken words are a question or an exclamation, then a question mark or exclamation mark is used instead of the comma [e.g. "What is your name?" asked the boy.]. Lessons 7 and 8

Heading and sub-heading

A **heading** is used to show the subject of the text that follows it [e.g. Staying healthy]. **Sub-headings** are used to show what each section or paragraph is about [e.g. Exercise; Diet]. Headings and sub-headings are used to organise ideas in writing.

Noun

Nouns are words that name things, people and places [e.g. car; park; man; day]. These are examples of **common nouns**.
- **Proper nouns** are the names of specific people, places, things [e.g. Joe Henson; Banbury Park; February]. Proper nouns start with a capital letter.
- A **noun phrase** is a group of words built around a noun. An expanded noun phrase might include a determiner, adjective[s], nouns and/or prepositional phrases [e.g. the fast police car with flashing lights]. Lessons 5 and 6
- A **compound noun** is a noun made up of two root words joined together [e.g. footpath, butterfly.].
- An **abstract noun** is a noun that does not describe a person, place or thing but rather names an idea, quality, or state [e.g. bravery; willingness]. These words are often formed by adding suffixes such as –ness to adjectives.
- A **collective noun** refers to a whole group of things [e.g. a class of children]. Lesson 15

Paragraph

A **paragraph** is a group of sentences that go together because they have one main idea or theme. Paragraphs are used to organise ideas in writing. Lessons 25 and 26

Phrase

A **phrase** is a group of words that are connected together. Lesson 1
- A **noun phrase** is a group of words built around a noun. An expanded noun phrase might include a determiner, adjective[s], nouns and/or prepositional phrases [e.g. the fast police car with flashing lights]. Lessons 5 and 6
- A **prepositional phrase** is a group of words starting with a preposition [e.g. in the morning; under the bridge]. Lesson 6

Prefix

A **prefix** is a group of letters added to the start of an existing word to make another word. Adding a prefix changes the meaning of the original word, for example changing the meaning of adjectives or verbs [e.g. unpleasant, dishonest; undo, reconnect, overload]. Grammar 5
- Some prefixes create negative meanings [e.g. undone; disagree]. Other prefixes have specific meanings [e.g. replay – 're–' means 'again'; submarine – 'sub–' means 'under']. Lesson 29

Preposition

A **preposition** is a word that shows how one thing relates to another in terms of place [e.g. <u>in</u> the bin; <u>behind</u> the tree; <u>from</u> the window], time [e.g. <u>before</u> dinner; <u>during</u> dinner; <u>after</u> dinner] or cause [e.g. <u>due to</u> the weather].

A preposition is always followed by a noun, pronoun or noun phrase and this creates a **prepositional phrase** [e.g. before breakfast; before him; before the storm]. Lesson 6

Some words, including 'before', can act as prepositions or conjunctions. They are prepositions if they are followed by a noun, pronoun or noun phrase. They are conjunctions if followed by a clause.

Pronoun

A **pronoun** is a word that stands in place of a noun, proper noun or noun phrase.
- **Personal pronouns** are the most commonly used pronouns [e.g. I/me; he/him; they/them]. They help to avoid repetition. Lessons 9 and 10
- **Possessive pronouns** are used to show possession [e.g. This pencil is <u>mine</u>. That painting is <u>hers</u>.]. Lesson 21
- **Relative pronouns** [who, whose, which, that] are used at the start of relative clauses. Grammar 5
- **Reflexive pronouns** are used to refer back to the subject [e.g. myself; himself]. Grammar 5
- **Indefinite pronouns** are used when the noun is unknown [e.g. someone]. Grammar 5
- Other words, such as **determiners**, can be used as pronouns if they stand in place of a noun [e.g. <u>This</u> is mine.]. Lesson 10

Overuse of pronouns can lead to confusion about who or what the pronoun refers to. Lesson 22

Sentence

A **sentence** is a group of words put together to say something that makes sense. A sentence starts with a capital letter and ends with a full stop [.], question mark [?] or exclamation mark [!]. A sentence may consist of one clause or more than one clause. Sentences can be made longer by adding words, phrases and clauses that give more detail. Lessons 1 and 2

There are different forms of sentence with different functions and different grammatical patterns.
- **Statements** give information. They usually start with a subject followed by a verb [e.g. Joe ran away.].
- **Questions** ask for information and need a response. They can be formed using a question word [e.g. <u>What</u> is the weather like today?], a subject–verb reversal [e.g. <u>Is it</u> cold today?] or a **question tag** [e.g. It is cold today, <u>isn't it?</u>]. Questions always end with a question mark. Lesson 28
- **Commands** direct someone to do something. The main clause starts with a verb [e.g. Come here.].
- **Exclamations** express strong emotions and always end with an exclamation mark. A strict definition of an exclamation refers to sentences starting with 'What' or 'How' [e.g. What a surprise! How amazing!]. However, **interjections** are also exclamatory [e.g. Oh dear!]. Exclamation marks are sometimes added to other sentences to make exclamatory statements [e.g. It was great!] or exclamatory commands [e.g. Stop right there!]. However, this does not change the form of the sentence.

A positive sentence can be made into a negative one by using negative words [e.g. no; not; never]. Lesson 27

Sentence punctuation

Sentence punctuation refers to the use of capital letters and full stops to show the boundaries between sentences. It is an important part of punctuation as it helps to make the meaning of a text clear.

- A **question mark [?]** is used in place of a full stop if a sentence is a question.
- An **exclamation mark [!]** is used for exclamations or to show strong feeling.
- **Capital letters** are also used at the start of proper nouns and for the word 'I'.

Singular and plural

Many nouns have **singular** and **plural** forms. Singular means just one; plural means more than one. Many plurals are formed by adding –s or –es to the singular noun [e.g. cats; dogs; fox<u>es</u>; lad<u>ies</u>]. However, some nouns have irregular plural forms [e.g. child – children; mouse – mice]. Some nouns are the same in the plural as they are in the singular [e.g. sheep; fish] and some nouns are always plural [e.g. scissors]. Non-countable nouns do not have a plural form [e.g. butter]. Lesson 15

Standard English

Standard English is the form of English usually used in writing or formal speech. Non-Standard English is used in informal or local speech. Non-Standard English is sometimes shown in the use of verb forms [e.g. 'I done it.' rather than 'I did it.'; 'We was late.' rather than 'We were late.']. Lessons 19 and 20 It can also be shown in the use of pronouns [e.g. 'me brother and me went' rather than 'my brother and I went'] and adverbs [e.g. 'He ran quick.' rather than 'He ran quickly.']. Other examples of non-Standard forms include double negatives. Grammar 5

Suffix

A **suffix** is a group of letters added to the end of an existing word to make another word. Suffixes often change words into different word classes. For example, they are used to form adjectives [e.g. wonder<u>ful</u>; power<u>less</u>; fam<u>ous</u>] or to form nouns [e.g. kind<u>ness</u>; entertain<u>ment</u>]. Lesson 29

Suffixes can also be used to form verbs. Grammar 5

Verb

A **verb** is a 'doing' or 'being' word [e.g. He <u>ran</u>. He <u>is</u> sad.]. Verbs are important because they tell us about the actions in a sentence. They also show tense.

- **Tense (past and present)** Verbs usually have a tense. The tense tells us *when* the action happened – in the past or present. Many past-tense verbs are formed by adding –ed [e.g. waited; stopped; hurried]. Some verbs have irregular past-tense forms [e.g. see/saw; forget/forgot]. Lessons 19 and 20
- **Progressive forms** [also called continuous forms] can be used in the present and past tense to describe events that are, or were, in progress for some time. They use the –ing form of the verb with the helper [or auxiliary] verb 'am/are/is' in the present tense or 'was/were' in the past tense [e.g. He <u>is</u> sing<u>ing</u>. She <u>was</u> walk<u>ing</u>.].
- **Perfect forms** are used to show time-and-cause relationships. The **present perfect form** of a verb is used to refer to events that began in the past but are still ongoing or still have consequences now [e.g. The tent has started to leak.]. It is formed using the helper [or auxiliary] verb 'has/have'. Lesson 20

Vowel and consonant

Vowels and **consonants** are the separate sounds that make up spoken words. In writing, these sounds are represented by letters or groups of letters. Lesson 4

Most of the letters in the alphabet represent consonant sounds. These are b c d f g h j k l m n p q r s t v w x y and z. Some vowel sounds are represented by the vowel letters a e i o and u. Other vowel sounds are represented by more than one letter [e.g. <u>ea</u>gle; <u>ar</u>m].

Word class

Every word belongs to a **word class**. The word class shows how the word is used. The main word classes are noun, verb, adjective, adverb, pronoun, conjunction, preposition and determiner. Lesson 3

- **Homonyms** are words that sound the same and are spelt the same but have different meanings. This means they can belong in different word classes. The context in which a word is used in a particular sentence determines its meaning and which word class it belongs to [e.g. He did <u>well</u>. He fetched water from the <u>well</u>.]. Lesson 3

Word family

Words in the same **word family** are related by meaning and how they are formed. They share the same root word [e.g. family, familiar] or a common root [e.g. horror, horrible]. Lesson 30

- A **root word** is a stand-alone word without any prefixes or suffixes added to it [e.g. 'build' is the root word of 'builder', 'rebuild', 'building']. Lesson 30